Creating Healthy Communities

A MODEL FOR LOCAL ACTION

GARY THEILEN PhD

Theilen Consulting

gtheilen@cox.net

Edited by Heather Hollen

Text and cover design by Carl Brune

Cover image by Nancy Sander

ISBN 979-8-218-34738-3

Printed in the USA

TABLE OF CONTENTS

ILLUSTRATIONS

CASE STUDIES

TEMPLATES

INTRODUCTION

This book highlights and provides many examples that illustrate the great potential of local, inclusive, volunteer-driven planning and action organizations in creating healthy communities. The definition of "healthy communities" used in this book is broad; it includes access to vital health care services, preventive services for healthy development, and other assets necessary for health, including safety, affordable housing, quality education, and income security. The following chapters provide a model for organizing and implementing local planning and action organizations that can provide leadership to ensure these assets are in place. The model is designed to be helpful to students, professionals, and community leaders who want to take action to meet critical needs in local communities. Each chapter contains case examples highlighting the adverse effects of local inaction and how community action (via forming inclusive local organizations) can help empower local leaders to respond effectively to community needs. Many of the examples in this book came from the Community Development Support Association (CDSA). I have used these examples for a variety of reasons. First, many professionals, students, and volunteer readers will be involved in start-up situations where they help to organize local planning and action. CDSA was a start-from-scratch organization developed with the basic model proposed in this book. Further, CDSA has been operating for over thirty years and has addressed (and continues to address) a broad range of local needs, including public transportation, early childhood development, youth employment and emergency assistance, and housing. The case examples illustrate how a organization was formed for volunteer-driven planning and action, as well as challenges faced and early successes. The book also provides case examples of established organizations whose primary function was to provide technical assistance for volunteer-driven planning and action. This book stresses the importance of local organizations that focus on the dual goals of achieving short-term *and* long-term improvements in health, education, and economic security, *and* inclusive engagement of local leaders to increase their confidence and capacity to bring about needed change.

I have been fortunate to work in diverse settings, including rural and urban, nonprofit and governmental, startup and existing organizations, and statewide, multi-county, and neighborhood organizations. The settings that have accounted for most of my experience include the Community Council of Central Oklahoma (Oklahoma City, OK), West Virginia University School of Social Work (Morgantown, WV), Community Development Support Association (Enid, OK), Oklahoma Commission on Children and Youth (Oklahoma City, OK), and Caring Communities Support Center (Edmond, OK). These settings and experiences are the bedrock for the organizational requirements and practice model proposed in this book. The practice model and methodology are designed to be helpful for both professional and volunteer leaders in various types of organizations, including community-wide planning and action organizations, neighborhood associations, and nonprofit direct service organizations that provide staff support for local community engagement in planning and integrating services for a specific population or need.

For context, I'd like to start with a brief overview of my background in each setting, highlighting the five community organization settings I've worked in throughout my career (beginning with my first). These settings illustrate the community's needs and challenges and how local planning and action organizations address them. The examples illustrate the lack of adequate local infrastructure to address deficiencies in many communities and the variety of resources that communities have deployed to develop that infrastructure.

COMMUNITY COUNCIL OF CENTRAL OKLAHOMA

Looking back on my career in community organization, I was very fortunate to have worked for the Community Council of Central Oklahoma as my first employer. I gained vital insights from this experience that were invaluable in guiding and motivating me throughout my career. The Council was a nonprofit planning and action agency that served the metropolitan area of Oklahoma City. Its broad goals were to improve health and economic security in the metro area through community research, planning, coordination, and action. The Council took on various community needs and services and was highly successful.

As a young person entering the field, I was greatly inspired. It felt incredible being part of a volunteer-driven nonprofit planning and action agency making significant strides in improving access to and quality of health care, increasing employment and training opportunities for low-income populations, and securing and redirecting financial resources to create an innovative organization that provided housing, education, and recreation opportunities for youth and families. The Executive Director was committed to community involvement and was highly effective at engaging a broad base of volunteer leaders who were "movers and shakers" in getting things done at the local level. The Board of Directors included business leaders, the Managing Editor of *The Oklahoman* (a major newspaper in the Oklahoma City metro area), leaders of faith-based organizations, physicians, minority group leaders, and local governmental leadership. Board members' contributions to the Council went well beyond attendance at monthly meetings. Several board members chaired major project committees (which met between board meetings). These committees addressed health, poverty, youth development, and other needs. Some board members chaired internal committees, which dealt with the challenges of the Council's multiple and changing funding sources and securing personnel to carry out projects.

Bringing about meaningful community changes frequently involved working with interest groups, some of which opposed changes in policy and allocation of resources. Board members led the way in influencing important community decisions by utilizing their access to decision-makers and other political resources. The Executive Director provided vital staff support to board members which included research on community needs/priorities and policy, program, and funding alternatives. During my six years with the Council, I served as a Graduate Intern, Assistant Director, Interim Director, and Director of Area-Wide Health Planning. The following is a brief summary of Council projects and achievements.

Public Health Funding

With Oklahoma City facing a public health funding crisis, the Council was instrumental in passing a bond issue that substantially increased funding for public health needs. Board leaders, including the Managing Editor of *The Oklahoman*, took the lead in accomplishing this objective.

Area-Wide Health Planning Agency

Recognizing the need to improve access, affordability, quality, and coordination of health care services to community residents, the Council applied for and secured funding and designation as the Area-Wide Health Planning Agency. The Council played a major role in designing and bringing partners together to create the University of Oklahoma Health Sciences Center. This collaboration brought together a wide range of public and private organizations on a single campus—including hospitals, the Oklahoma State Health Department, health research and education organizations, and the Oklahoma State Department of Mental Health. The Area-Wide Health Planning Agency acted to maintain and increase access and affordability of health care to residents with low incomes. The Council took the lead in helping secure federal

Community Action funds for a family medicine clinic in an inner city low-income area, thus providing affordable primary care to residents. The Agency also took steps to guide the development of new health facilities in the area in ways that didn't undercut the capacity of existing nonprofits to maintain the charity care they were already providing. In a period of concerns about creating excessive numbers of hospital beds and grossly inadequate state and federal funding for charity care, the Agency successfully opposed the construction of an additional for-profit hospital that wouldn't offer charity care and would potentially "cream off" paying patients—thus, undercutting the capacity of existing nonprofits to serve at-risk populations.

Economic Opportunities and Access to Services for Low-Income Populations

Recognizing the need to address poverty, the Council applied for and received federal "War on Poverty" funding. Over the years, this brought millions of dollars into the area to fund employment, early childhood education, health, and housing programs. The Community Action programs engaged leaders of low-income populations in forming neighborhood councils to guide and provide feedback on neighborhood needs and actions required to deal with them. The Council created a community-wide Action Board, which included neighborhood leaders and broader community leaders in planning and acting to reduce poverty.

Creation of the Neighborhood Service Organization

This innovative nonprofit agency continues to provide a wide range of housing, health care, and family support services to inner city youth and families. As noted below, it was initially funded through redirection of funds from two neighborhood services agencies—one funded by the United Way and the other through faith-based funding. Since its inception, this innovative new agency has greatly expanded services and resources for financing, facilities, and partnerships to serve inner city needs.

This initiative began when the United Way asked the Council to conduct a study of an existing United Way-funded neighborhood services agency. This study was requested due to concerns about unheeded Budget Committee recommendations. The concerns included low numbers of people being served by the agency, quality of services offered, and lack of advocacy initiatives on behalf of the neighborhood. The Council Board referred the United Way request to the Council's Neighborhood Services Committee, for which I provided staff support.

The Neighborhood Services Committee coordinated the study, which confirmed the concerns and inaction of the agency. The Committee recommended ending funding for the agency and reallocating funds in a way that improved the breadth and quality of services offered as well as serving expanded numbers of youth and families. As part of the study, the Committee identified a faith-based neighborhood service organization assisting other inner city neighborhoods whose capacity was hampered by insufficient resources. The Committee also secured information from other communities with innovative and productive approaches to serving neighborhood needs. The Committee reached out to the board members of the faith-based program to see if they might be willing to combine resources to create a new agency to help meet broad inner city needs. The new agency would be led by a Board of Directors, which would be more inclusive of neighborhood leadership and community leaders. Faith-based organization representatives agreed but said they would need permission from the national body and asked for our assistance. I traveled to New York with the faith-based board representatives to do this. The nationwide organization liked the proposal and approved it. The Neighborhood Services Committee led the implementation of this collaboration, and the Neighborhood Service Organization was "born." All parties to this collaboration were excited about the new partnership. There were many challenges to be tackled in the early stage of development, but the long-term benefits were very productive.

WEST VIRGINIA UNIVERSITY SCHOOL OF SOCIAL WORK

Late in my tenure with the Council, I received an unexpected call from my former advisor at the University of Oklahoma. He had become Dean of the West Virginia School of Social Work and was calling to offer me a research faculty job. At the time, I had just been appointed Director of Area-Wide Health Planning and felt it would undermine the program if I left abruptly. I thanked him for the offer and told him that if a position ever opened to teach community organization, I would seriously consider it. (Since West Virginia is a rural state with unique needs, the School decided to specialize in services to rural communities and had a student body that was highly interested in this specialization. The Dean knew of my rural background and felt I could contribute significantly as a faculty member.) About a year later, I received another call from the Dean saying that a community organization teaching position had become available. My roles would include both classroom teaching and supervision of graduate internships. I was excited about the opportunity and felt my experience could benefit the program. Following interviews with faculty and students, I accepted the position. As I began my employment, I realized that there was considerable turbulence in West Virginia. For example, I was told that a student at the School and her family had recently been murdered. The family supported Miners for Democracy, an organization active in union reform. Coal is a significant industry in the state, and health hazards, safety concerns, and external ownership of assets received considerable attention from activists seeking change.

Moreover, infrastructure in West Virginia for community and neighborhood planning and action to improve health and economic well-being was notably lacking, and few Community Action initiatives were in place. However, there were two exceptions. The Compensative Extension Agency had taken the lead in establishing the Appalachian Center initiative to help address local needs. While the Cooperative Extension Service (historically associated with research, demonstration projects, technical assistance to improve agriculture production, and youth programs for rural populations) initially had a more limited scope, the Appalachian Center had a broader focus on the full range of community needs. These vast needs called for increased empowerment of local West Virginia communities.

About six months after I arrived, a group of students asked to meet with me to discuss a possible approach for integrating classroom and internship learning. I agreed, and as time passed, my belief in "mining" the wisdom of consumers in policy-making and program development was affirmed. As I got to know the students, I found out they felt they were only getting a portion of what they came for and expected to learn in the program. These students sought ways to make a difference and improve the environment, ensure health and mental health services in rural areas, reduce health and safety hazards in mines, and improve economic opportunities in rural areas. They were earnest about change and, for the most part, were willing to help do the work to accomplish it.

The students who approached me expressed deep frustration with what they perceived as a disconnect between what they were studying in the classroom and the knowledge and skills they needed to address the needs of West Virginia communities. They sought an education model that integrated actual theory and practical models to prepare them to empower local leaders, meet needs, and allocate resources. Their message was, "If this School is meant to be a leader in innovation to meet rural needs, we need to start with innovation in the school's education program." Initially, they wanted me to continue teaching a course in community organization practice, supervise internships, and work with students to accomplish local objectives. These students realized the need for continuity in service to communities and that student internships generally lasted no more than two semesters. They believed that the incoming group of graduate students was large enough to maintain the programs and achieve continuity. However, a faculty member would be needed to facilitate the successful transition of student services to communities throughout the life of the projects. We worked together to develop a detailed proposal for review and approval by the Dean. He liked the idea, and we began implementation. We named the new venture the Rural Community Development Learning Center. The first rural community development project we initiated is discussed below.

Health Project Recruiting Physicians in Preston County, West Virginia

In conducting a preliminary assessment of community needs, we learned that Preston County had a shortage of physicians and had been unable to make progress on recruitment. We approached Appalachian Center leadership about a cooperative endeavor to address this. Their response was positive, and they suggested we contact the county extension leader in Kingwood, West Virginia, about participating in a joint venture. We met with the County Extension Agent, who was very supportive and aware of the shortage of physicians. We agreed upon a plan. The School would establish an internship with the county office, the county extension leader would provide day-to-day site supervision, and there would be regular meetings of students with the county leader and myself as the academic supervisor.

A Preston County Health Planning Committee comprised of volunteer leaders and local health care providers was appointed to guide the project. Students contacted the National Health Service Corp about possible funding and assistance recruiting physicians. The students then wrote a grant request to the National Health Service Corp, which was approved. The project successfully recruited and retained physicians, and student assistance to the Health Planning Committee continued for years. The physician recruitment project also helped the local hospital and health department to achieve their objectives in serving the health needs of local residents.

The Rural Community Development Learning Center initiated and staffed many additional projects. These projects dealt with community water, roads, mental health, and environmental protection needs. The Center also established potential roles for the University in providing infrastructure to support community development and training professionals to work in rural communities.

While I enjoyed teaching, supervising interns, and conducting research during my eight years at West Virginia University, I also missed direct work with community leadership as a central feature of my career. At the time, I was completing my PhD at the University of Pittsburgh, which included research on the development and use of political resources in influencing decision-making. At the time, our family regretted the distance from our extended family. I contemplated being self-employed and doing community organization as a volunteer leader. I decided to expand the family business near Enid, Oklahoma (my father was retiring) and pursue a volunteer leadership role.

Our family made the move, and after putting critical features of the business in place, I worked with local leaders to conduct a key informant survey. I interviewed about twenty-five local leaders to learn their thoughts about community strengths, weaknesses, and critical improvements. I also explored their views about the need for an organization to address these needs and their willingness to participate. (The method for developing a key informant survey is discussed in Chapter III). In Chapters III and IV, this work, which led to the creation of the Community Development Support Association (CDSA), is discussed in detail. In addition, I've also included project illustrations detailing actions taken to establish public transportation and improve access to and quality of health care for low-income families. I have used these illustrations because this "start from scratch" initiative has provided (and continues to provide) leadership, resulting in improved outcomes for more than thirty years. CDSA exemplifies the great need and potential for the local model proposed in the book.

CDSA has responded to local needs by securing funding for and developing evidence-based early childhood programs, providing housing for low- and middle-income families, providing youth employment opportunities, and improving access to and quality of health care. Aided by the strategic assistance of an Oklahoma State Senator whose district included the Enid area, CDSA took leadership in securing funding for and initiating an evidence-based early childhood education program: Parents as Teachers. The organization has accomplished these objectives due to the passionate work of local leaders (supported by dedicated and highly skilled program and fiscal staff and four executive directors with unique insights for achieving goals) and the generous support of a grateful community.

The Oklahoma Commission on Children and Youth is a state agency that monitors child service agencies, particularly those providing services related to child abuse, neglect, and juvenile offenses. A second function of the agency is to support services to prevent child neglect, abuse, and juvenile crimes. The Commission had established about forty County Partnership Boards to help communities strengthen their services. While serving as CDSA Executive Director, I received a call from the State Senator who had provided leadership in CDSA efforts to develop early childhood services in the Enid area and throughout the state. The Executive Director of the Oklahoma Commission on Children and Youth was at the Senator's home in Enid. They were discussing the Commission's Partnership Boards, and the Senator believed it would be helpful for the Director to hear about CDSA's model for local planning and action. I was glad to have this opportunity and met with the Commission's Executive Director and the Senator to discuss CDSA's approach and accomplishments.

A couple of months later, the Executive Director called and asked me to provide consultation to the Commission. We reached an agreement, and I began visits to County Partnership Boards to learn what their objectives were and help make progress in achieving them. As a whole, the Boards were improving communication among agencies, which was both helpful to members of the groups and the communities they served. However, achievements and significant improvements in programs or securing new resources were sometimes limited. Several factors contributed to this problem. Partnership Board membership was mostly limited to agency staff members and few or no participants who were volunteer leaders. Another inhibiting factor was the limited staff support the Commission could provide to the County Partnership Boards. For the forty Boards scattered across the state, at times only one or two individuals were available to provide staff support. I recommended that the Commission identify some pilot sites to contribute intensive staff support and utilize the basic model outlined in this book. The Commission agreed, and pilot sites were identified. A few of those sites and their achievements are briefly discussed below.

Texas County Partnership Board

Texas County in Oklahoma is a rural county located a considerable distance from the state capitol and state-funded family and youth services providers. The Texas County Partnership Board was designated as a pilot site and as a result received intensive staff support in addressing local needs. The Board secured state funding for a locally governed child and family service agency, significantly improving the quality of services available to local families. The Texas County Partnership Board also took the lead in securing a Federally Qualified Health Center. The partnership serves as the Community Health Improvement Organization (CHIO) for the County and surrounding area. (This was possible because the Texas County Board had achieved nonprofit status.)

Pottawatomie and Lincoln County Collaboration

Pottawatomie and Lincoln Counties in Oklahoma experienced many challenges, including high child neglect and abuse rates and issues impeding school success. The Pottawatomie Child Welfare Collaborative and the Lincoln County Partnership for Child Wellbeing acted and formed school health teams that provided children and families access to counseling, health services, and other services to support school success.

CARING COMMUNITIES SUPPORT CENTER

Seeing communities make notable strides in improving local health, education, and income security outcomes, a former colleague and I discussed the question, "Could we develop a nonprofit whose primary function was providing in-community consultation in building inclusive, effective planning and action organizations?" We decided it was possible and began organizing a pilot project to provide in-community consultation and support for developing local infrastructure. After consulting with leaders and professionals we had previously worked with, we formed a steering committee and subsequent Board of Directors comprised of volunteer leaders passionate about local improvement. Initially, our funding came from our annual fundraiser, a local foundation, and fee-for-service income from communities. The following are a few examples of Caring Communities Support Center projects.

Community Action Program in Central Oklahoma

The Avedis Foundation, located in Shawnee, Oklahoma, had received an application for assistance from the Central Oklahoma Community Action Agency. The Agency, which had a budget of $3 million annually and provided many vital services to a six-county area, was in severe financial trouble and close to losing its federal funding. The Avedis Foundation staff approached the Caring Communities Support Center about doing an agency study with recommendations on how to put the Agency on sound financial and program footing. Having served as the Executive Director of a Community Action Agency, I was aware of the importance of the Agency's service to the county. Services included:

- Public transportation
- Housing repair
- Affordable housing rentals
- Case management services for families with family emergencies
- Assistance applying for earned-income tax credits

The Caring Committee Board approved our involvement with the project. Avedis communicated that if the Central Oklahoma Community Action Agency implemented study recommendations and was in a sound position, it would consider additional funding. I began the study by interviewing all board members, key staff, funders, and community leaders and conducting a detailed financial and program analysis. Midway into the study, I realized that the Agency would fail without immediate corrective action. I made regular monthly reports to the Board. Board members told me they were enthusiastic that they were finally getting some help. They decided to employ me as an Interim Director to help lead them through the crisis.

Caring Communities Support Center's involvement with the project lasted for about two years. The work was intense and challenging. The Central Oklahoma Community Action Board had not had sound executive leadership for a long time and felt helpless to solve the problem. Qualified fiscal staff were lacking, some transportation vehicles needed repairs, and unpaid debt was a significant problem. Relationships with funders and communities had gone downhill. With the helpful support of Avedis and the Oklahoma Department of Commerce, we strengthened and reengaged the Board, paid the debt, secured a much improved facility, employed qualified fiscal and executive staff, and rebuilt confidence with funders. The Agency also invested in an evidence-based early childhood program, which had shown great promise. In addition, the Caring Communities Support Center gained knowledge about the loaned staff alternative to serve existing nonprofits.

Step-Up Program for Homeless Youth

Leaders in the Weatherford and Clinton area identified housing, education, employment, and other support services for homeless youth as a priority unmet need, and they requested help from the Caring Communities Support Center.

We conducted a key informant survey of leaders in the two communities as the foundation for developing a plan of action. Caring Communities Support Center recognized the day-to-day staff support required to form a new program. CCSC provided funds to employ a local person to organize Steering Committee meetings and follow up on decisions. Community enthusiasm for action on this need was great. The Step-Up Program applied for and received nonprofit status, held a successful fundraiser, employed staff, and began providing homeless youth with housing, counseling, and help with education and employment. The organization has many success stories in serving youth. Community enthusiasm for the program has led to annual funding from a nonprofit thrift shop in the area and individual and business donors, as well as funding through an annual fundraiser.

Healthy Steps Early Childhood Program

Leaders in the Stillwater, Oklahoma, area sought assistance to replace and expand Healthy Steps, an early childhood program provided in collaboration with the pediatric clinic at the Stillwater Medical Center. The Oklahoma State Department of Health previously funded Healthy Steps, and parents, pediatricians, and early childhood specialists were excited about the contributions to child health made possible by the program. However, to the community's dismay, the Health Department discontinued funding. Caring Communities Support Center provided consultation and funds for part-time local staff services to the Payne County Early Childhood Coalition to gain funding and expand the program. Due to the leadership provided by the Coalition and support from Caring Communities Support Center, funding for a full-time early childhood specialist was provided through a combination of funds from a local foundation, Stillwater Medical Center, Central Oklahoma Community Action Program, and an annual fundraiser. The Coalition also provided leadership in developing other early childhood programs for the region.

LOOKING FORWARD

As the reader will note in the many examples provided above, local planning and action organizations are vital in addressing community needs. These organizations can lead the way in taking action to improve health, education, and economic security outcomes for all citizens, especially for the most vulnerable in our communities.

Creating Healthy Communities

The Case for Greater Investment in Local Community Planning and Action Organizations

COMMUNITY (THE PLACE) MATTERS

There is increasing awareness that growth and economic success in a community or region frequently leaves sizable populations behind (Atkins, 2021). This can lead to tragic consequences for the people affected and also for the larger population as a whole. These consequences can include diminished health, crime, a weakened workforce, and social division. The COVID-19 pandemic was a painful and enduring reminder of this reality.

Central to these consequences is the failure of local communities and neighborhoods to provide vital opportunities for families and individuals to achieve healthy development. When these opportunities are insufficient or nonexistent, individuals and families suffer costly and complex barriers to healthy growth, impacting the entire community. Furthermore, these negative conditions may be self-sustaining.

The lack of vital opportunities in many local communities calls for more effective civic engagement, planning, and action to improve community health and income security outcomes.

Critical Place-Based Opportunities

ECONOMIC OPPORTUNITIES

- *education and training*
- *employment opportunities*
- *livable income*

SAFETY

- *safe and supportive neighborhoods*
- *law enforcement*
- *healthy community environments*

MUTUAL SUPPORT

- *healthy family system*
- *access to health care*
- *community services*
- *education programs for at-risk youth*

SOCIALIZATION

- *community norms supporting individuals and families*
- *education for youth and adults*
- *faith-based organizations*
- *opportunities to participate in democratic decision-making*

Individuals and families that lack personal support systems may not be able to achieve emotional stability and/or economic sufficiency. Publicly and privately financed programs may not achieve their objectives to make needed changes because they lack community feedback and/or participation. Local citizens (including youth) do not learn that their participation can change local conditions and outcomes. Community apathy, inaction, and despair become the norm in crucial areas of community life. This despair can contribute to drug use and various health issues.

In a recent article in the Stanford Social Innovation Review, the authors stress the value of place-based opportunities that address the causes of inequity and increased opportunities for health and well-being. The article cites research confirming that many communities are economically disadvantaged and lack the human capacity for effective local planning and grant writing, including the ability to mobilize internal resources and secure external resources. The article includes examples of how foundations have funded local initiatives that simultaneously helped build local capacity and improve health and income security (Atkins, 2021). Similarly, the community examples provided in this book illustrate over and over the consequences of insufficient local infrastructure.

Lack of economic, safety, mutual assistance, and socialization opportunities can interact to maintain adverse outcomes in communities.

CASE STUDY #1
Lack of Vital Opportunities Necessitates Local Action

The Oklahoma Commission on Children and Youth worked with a group of concerned leaders in the Northwest 10th Street area of Oklahoma City to create an advocacy organization (Friends of Northwest 10th Street) to address problems related to sustained poverty facing the local population.

One of Friends of Northwest 10th Street's first tasks was conducting a key informant survey of educational leaders (e.g., school management, teachers, and parent-teacher groups), faith-based organizations, and neighborhood providers.

Survey of leaders (including business leaders, school administrators and teachers, faith-based organizations, volunteer leaders of parent-teacher groups, health agencies, and emergency assistant agencies) indicated that many families had insufficient incomes to secure safe and standard housing. Moreover, if those residents could find housing, many could not maintain rental payments, leading to frequent moves. Frequent moves interrupted the continuity of their children's education.

Crime and safety issues impacted the willingness of businesses to move into the area. One leader who operated an event center in the area and had completed an expensive renovation was shocked to learn of two murders in an apartment building across the Street. Police protection was deemed to be insufficient by both residents and businesses. Safety factors also contributed to resident mobility. Many residents lacked a "medical home" and primary care physician. These residents depended on emergency rooms for health care, lacking continuity of care.

Opportunities for youth to participate in fitness and character development programs were limited. Parent opportunities to participate in education and parenting programs were limited, as was childcare. Opportunities for residents to participate in organizations advocating for improvements in local conditions were also unavailable. The weight of the multitudes of opportunity shortfalls seemed insurmountable for residents and leaders.

With assistance from the Oklahoma Commission on Children and Youth staff, local leaders created Friends of Northwest 10th Street, which successfully improved safety, adult education, youth fitness and character-building programs, health services, and other opportunities within the area.

Many communities face urgent problems now, with nothing on the horizon to address them.

WAITING FOR ACTION FROM STATE AND NATIONAL LEVELS CAN BE COSTLY FOR LOCAL RESIDENTS

Many communities face urgent problems now, with nothing on the horizon to address them. Issues include:

- Lack of access to affordable and quality health care
- Lack of affordable housing
- Unsafe neighborhoods
- Lack of sufficient income for basic needs
- Failing schools
- Drug abuse and mental illness

Unaddressed broad needs at state and national levels make local action critical. Communities must take action to address these needs at the local level and to build grassroots demand for change at the state and federal levels. Currently, serious issues at the state and national levels impair the capability of

THE CASE FOR GREATER INVESTMENT IN LOCAL COMMUNITY PLANNING & ACTION ORGANIZATIONS

communities to improve outcomes. Divisiveness, disinformation, and lack of leadership can lead the public to lose faith in the government and other major institutions' ability to address threats to citizen well-being. The case examples used in this book represent a lack of these opportunities.

COMMUNITIES RECEIVE MULTIPLE BENEFITS FROM EFFECTIVE LOCAL ACTION

Effective broad-based and inclusive engagement of local citizens at neighborhood and community levels in planning and action to improve local conditions *provides a way to help ensure critical opportunities are available.* Local participation can lead to multiple community benefits:

- Addressing critical, immediate needs
- Empowering citizens to influence important decisions and gain skills and confidence through inclusion in community action organizations
- Reviving trust in democratic institutions and processes
- Positioning local leaders to impact the allocation and efficacy of existing state and federal resources
- Achieving continuity of funding and services by bridging changes in political administrations, funding cutbacks, or addressing changes in public or private agency policies
- Creating new employment opportunities through the establishment or expansion of services, housing, and education
- Providing accurate feedback to organizations administering services that require adjustments to fulfill the community's needs adequately

Properly conceived and implemented local citizen-driven nonprofit planning and action organizations (that are inclusive, properly staffed, and sustained) can provide urban and rural communities a powerful vehicle to improve community health outcomes and income security.

CHAPTER II

Core Features of Inclusive Local Planning and Action Organizations

In presenting core features, I will draw heavily on more than fifty years of experience in community organization, as well as knowledge gained from professional education, scholarly articles, and lessons learned from volunteer leaders and professional colleagues.

Over the years, I have been fortunate to work as a community organizer in a wide range of settings, including:

Rural Grassroots

- Organizing and managing the Community Development Support Association
- Teaching community organization and supervising graduate students in rural development projects at West Virginia University School of Social Work
- Consulting with the Community Action Agency of Central Oklahoma

Urban Planning

- Community Council of Central Oklahoma
- Director of Comprehensive Health Planning Program

State Agencies

- Oklahoma Commission on Children and Youth (consultation with County and Community Partnership Boards)

In every community project, we faced significant challenges and, at times, seemingly insurmountable obstacles in achieving our goals and objectives. These included apathy and doubt that anything could be accomplished, resistance from some established institutions and decision-makers, an apparent lack of resources, and securing an existing agency capable of managing a "best practice" program with fidelity, even when we could secure the resources.

Yet, time and time again, the vast majority of the local civic planning and action organizations faced the challenges and found within themselves the energy and sense of empowerment to achieve small victories (and then larger ones) in making community opportunities available. In walking side by side with leaders and supporting them in achieving their objectives, my belief in the necessity and power of local civic engagement was greatly reinforced. Further, these experiences provided countless lessons on how to get things done in local communities.

The following is a summary of what my experiences with local leaders and volunteers have led me to hypothesize are the core features of local planning and action organizations.

GOVERNANCE OF LOCAL PLANNING AND ACTION ORGANIZATIONS IS INCLUSIVE AND VOLUNTEER-DRIVEN

To be clear, the proposed local planning and action organizations are nonprofits. The Boards of Directors of these organizations are made up primarily of volunteer leaders passionate about meeting critical local needs. These individuals believe in local civic engagement as a necessary avenue for "getting things done" to solve problems and reach goals. Leaders of major population groups affected by system deficiencies must be well-represented, along with leaders of crucial community-wide constituencies, including civic, human services, faith-based, and political leaders. Volunteer leaders of service providers can be a critical part of these organizations when these leaders are willing to put community needs ahead of agency gains.

Many communities (rural and urban) experience chronic inaction on critical deficiencies in health, education, and income security. In some of these communities, existing public and private entities are researching and taking action to deal with a portion of these deficiencies, but significant gaps remain. The community case examples in this book illustrate the shortfalls in both rural and urban communities. Existing governmental and private organizations may agree that needs exist but believe they lack the resources and political support to address the gaps. In other instances, these organizations oppose needed change. Inclusive volunteer-driven planning and action organizations can bring vital assets to these communities. These assets are discussed below.

Volunteer-Driven Planning and Action Organizations Can Act "Now"

The primary focus of inclusive planning and action organizations is to conduct community studies, including interviews with leaders from a full range of constituencies in the community, involve leaders in identifying priority needs,

Engage volunteer leaders who are passionate about local needs to serve on committees and/or the Board of Directors.

and take action to address these needs. Many volunteer board members and individuals interviewed in the study are passionate about dealing with one or more identified priorities. These priorities often require changes in policies, programs, and allocation of resources by public and private organizations. Volunteer-driven planning and action organizations can pursue these changes when public officials may be constrained by concerns about losing political support or when private organizations may be reluctant due to fears of losing funding or draining resources needed for direct services.

Inclusive Engagement from Diverse and Complementary Volunteer Leadership to Achieve Goals

The leadership includes:

- Leaders and consumer groups impacted by deficiencies in opportunities
- Leaders with program and policy knowledge
- Leaders with knowledge and linkages helpful in influencing decisions

This inclusive and diverse knowledge is invaluable in achieving desired outcomes. Volunteer-driven planning and action organizations can complement and strengthen the capacities of existing public and private leaders of entities that support needed change. In building diverse coalitions that provide feedback to existing organizations and alternative solutions to chronic problems, they offer leadership support to leaders and organizations that desire change but have faced internal and external resistance. In addition, planning and action organizations take the lead in building public and private partnerships to fund and deliver innovative direct service programs that improve community wellbeing.

This book focuses on planning and action by two primary types of organizations: (a) communities and neighborhoods that address the *full scope* of human service sectors (e.g., health, economic security, recreation, and others) with leaders that identify priorities and necessary interactions among sectors to provide vital opportunities to local residents and (b) existing nonprofits and public agencies that seek broad community engagement in planning and action in specific sectors (e.g., health, youth services, and income security).

Recruiting leadership that can play important roles in these organizations can be challenging but is clearly worth the effort. Leaders may face time constraints, competing commitments, and financial or childcare limitations. Finding workable times and places for meetings and dealing with the scope

Volunteer-driven planning and action organizations can complement and strengthen existing entities and leaders that support needed change.

of responsibilities that each leader can reasonably perform is essential. The organization needs to offer reimbursement for expenses, such as transportation, which may otherwise be excessively burdensome for participants.

ORGANIZATIONS TAKE ACTION TO SECURE IMPROVED OUTCOMES FOR COMMUNITIES

For good reasons, a vital component in recruiting key leaders is the organization's reputation for "getting things done." Too often, volunteers have been recruited into an organization with the promise of excellent results, which failed to materialize. The barriers to achieving desired outcomes are frequently immense, yet small but significant achievements lead to lessons learned and hope regenerated. Local organizations have avenues for action to improve results. These include:

- Providing "input" into the decision-making processes of organizations that allocate health, education, and welfare resources. This input includes advocating for policy changes where needed

- Securing and managing resources to fill gaps in community services

- Securing joint action by a variety of organizations to provide and integrate services around specific needs and populations.

- Developing, delivering, and evaluating innovative solutions to complex problems and introducing evidence-based programs and policies to meet local needs.

An organization that has a record of achieving objectives and includes organizational participants who have a track record of getting things done, supports the retention of members and the recruitment of additional leaders, partners, and financial resources. Bringing together this kind of team is a significant step in creating hope, excitement, and real possibilities for meeting challenges ahead.

Subsequent chapters address developing an organizational structure and staff support to maximize opportunities for making full and effective use of competencies provided by leaders.

An organization with a record of achieving objectives is more likely to retain members and recruit additional leaders, partners, and financial resources for current and future projects.

ORGANIZATIONAL COMPOSITION INCLUDES "KEY" COMPETENCIES

Organizations need technical and political resources to decide which problems to attack, how to solve the issues, and how to influence service provider decisions. If residents expect their local action to solve community problems effectively, the organization must have the competencies to do so. Organization composition should include persons with three primary kinds of competencies.

1. Members who know from direct experience the unmet needs or problems. These can include leaders of consumer groups, agency staff, administrators with direct experience in dealing with community needs, and politicians whose constituents have stressed the desire for action on specific issues.

2. Members with technical skills in analyzing the problem and creating alternative solutions. Agency staff with a history of putting programs together that respond effectively to community needs can be helpful here. University researchers or specialists who know best practices can make contributions. Volunteer leaders and/or professionals with experience introducing new ideas and programs into the community can also be helpful.

3. Members who can help secure access and help influence decision-makers in pivotal public and private organizations. These individuals can serve in various capacities, including the Board of Directors, Committees, Partners, and other supportive roles.

STAFF SUPPORT IS PROVIDED FOR ORGANIZATIONS

While the organization's decisions and actions are volunteer-driven, the organization's effectiveness will be greatly enhanced through the skilled performance of staff support functions. These functions can range from helping and working with leaders to prepare agendas, to writing minutes and proposals for funding, to helping the organization develop strategies to influence decision-makers. A detailed discussion of staff support is provided in Chapter 7.

What a planning and action organization needs most from volunteer leaders is leadership in defining needs, deciding courses of action, and influencing external decision-makers, which are vital to the community's well-being. However, volunteers often have many other demands for their time (e.g., family,

The availability of skilled staff support allows volunteers to focus on leadership functions.

CORE FEATURES OF INCLUSIVE LOCAL PLANNING AND ACTION ORGANIZATIONS employment, and participation in other organizations). The availability of skilled staff support allows volunteers to focus on leadership functions.

ORGANIZATIONS CREATE AND USE STRUCTURE TO ENHANCE PARTICIPATION AND PRODUCTIVITY

As Jo Freeman points out in her essay "The Tyranny of Structurelessness," properly designed organizational structure enhances participation by clarifying how decisions are made and providing avenues for members to participate effectively (Freeman, 1972). The structure should expedite progress toward achieving objectives. Using a committee process for detailed study and discussion of finance, personnel, and program issues gives the organization's Board or steering committee ample time and information to make decisions in multiple areas. Board staff roles and responsibilities must be clearly understood. Collaborative relationships with partner organizations must also be straightforward and mutually productive.

ORGANIZATIONS DEVELOP LINKAGES TO ACHIEVE MULTIPLE OBJECTIVES

Producing and sustaining improved community outcomes is a huge undertaking. The organization will need to influence decision-makers on policy and allocation of resources, secure information on evidenced-based practices, and find or develop qualified service delivery capacities. The good news is that there are usually multiple public and private organizations (as well as individual leaders within the community) with common or closely related objectives to those of the planning and action organization. A significant function of the organization's volunteer leadership and staff will be finding, securing, and maintaining linkages to achieve goals and objectives. This is time-consuming and challenging work. Yet, it's also exciting work since it builds a more extensive and robust base for change.

CONDUCTING ONGOING RESEARCH ON COMMUNITY NEEDS, PRIORITIES, BEST PRACTICES, AND OUTCOMES

From the beginning of citizen engagement, we are researching what residents view as pressing needs, what they think should be done, who should be involved to help influence decisions, and whether or not survey participants want to be part of an organizing initiative. We need information on best practices and—once policies and programs are established—how they are working. This information must be shared with residents, the organization's leaders, partners, funders, and governmental leadership. Further, we need continuous feedback from residents on programs and new priorities that may be emerging. This information contributes to reasons for celebrating and modifying organizational initiatives when necessary. It's also crucial for the organization's partners and funders as evidence of changes accomplished. Feedback is vital to the organization's health, relevance, and sustainability.

Feedback is vital.

ORGANIZATIONS SUSTAIN POSITIVE OUTCOMES

One of the great strengths of a volunteer-led civic engagement organization is that the organization can help "bridge" positive outcomes that otherwise may be at risk due to changing political administrations, changes in financing policies of governmental agencies and foundations, and economic ups and downs within a geographic area. Lack of sustainability can have dire consequences for neighborhood and community residents and partner organizations and weaken the local planning and action organization itself. Therefore, organizations must begin preparing ways to sustain positive change as part of their initial planning and maintain ongoing attention to this requirement as the project proceeds.

CHAPTER III

A Model for Community Empowerment to Improve Local Health, Education, and Income Security Outcomes

The following is an overview of essential and interacting elements of a model which local planning and action organizations can utilize to accomplish the dual overarching goals of:

- Achieving short- and long-term improvements in health and income security
- Strengthening the capacity of local leaders and organizations to participate effectively in improving community well-being

The process elements listed below are sequential and concurrent activities. The following is a detailed discussion of how core characteristics of planning and action organizations (such as volunteer governance, inclusiveness, and proper staff support and planning for sustainability) help to achieve desired outcomes. Community examples are provided to illustrate how the model processes contribute to local success in addressing needs.

MODEL PROCESS COMPONENTS

A. Inclusive involvement of local leaders in

B. Setting goals and

C. Building an organization which uses a

D. Problem-solving process to establish objectives, and

E. Political resources, and

F. Technical capacity to bring about changes in

G. Decision-making on programs, policies, and resource allocation to

H. Achieve desired community outcomes.

In this chapter, we'll explore the first two processes (A and B) of the model. Subsequent chapters deal with processes (C) through (H) above.

INCLUSIVE INVOLVEMENT OF LOCAL LEADERS

This phase is the "bedrock" to the totality of the process; the organization's priority emphasis on early, inclusive, and effective engagement of local leaders is critical to every step in the process because:

- Local leaders bring direct knowledge of needs and barriers facing residents, community assets for solving problems, and possible solutions
- The organization sends the message through its action on "Day 1" that its governance is volunteer-driven
- Local leaders can help mobilize constituencies to support a broad and influential coalition
- Opportunities are diminished for a "divide and conquer" strategy by external actors who are opposed to change

Initial Steps to Engage Local Leaders

Looking back at project successes, it is clear that listening and "mining local wisdom" were central to the success of these local projects. In most communities, we began with key informant interviews with local leaders and small groups.

STEP 1: KEY INFORMANT SURVEY

One tool I have found exceptionally helpful in the early stages of engaging leaders is the Key Informant Survey. This can be a powerful tool because it starts with a fundamental step—listening to many people who have vital information to share but sometimes feel they have not been truly heard.

KEY INFORMANT INTERVIEWS

The key informant approach is a research method for identifying and analyzing issues. It involves carefully identifying a select group of individuals (e.g., formal and informal leaders, influential people, and experts) and conducting in-depth interviews with them (Key Informant, 2017). The method is characteristic of interpretive qualitative research and ethnographic field research (Faifua, 2014).

Reasons to Conduct Key Informant Interviews

 Helps you to determine what leaders consider to be the strengths and weaknesses of community programs. This can lead to discussion about policies needed to improve community health, education, and income security.

 Provides insight into what actions leaders feel should be taken to deal with needs and issues in the community.

 Helps you identify leaders and individuals considered to be "movers and shakers" in getting things done in the community.

 Helps you identify leaders involved with similar issues in the community who might be committed to addressing current problems.

 Helps you determine whether or not the interviewees might be willing to participate in an organized effort to address the current problems they identified.

Key Informant Survey Design Process

1

PURPOSE

Identify the specific study purpose and the information you want to collect.

2

QUESTIONS

Formulate study questions. The questions should relate to the specific concerns of the study. Limit them to five or fewer. Use open-ended questions to encourage free discussion.

3

INTERVIEW GUIDE

Prepare a short interview guide listing significant topics and issues to be covered under each study question.

The purpose of the Key Informant Survey is to get initial information which can provide guidance on what community leaders (leaders and groups impacted by opportunity deficiencies and leaders in the community as a whole) view as priorities for action. In addition, the survey can identify persons viewed as "movers and shakers" in getting things accomplished at the community level. Further, participants can assist the organization in mapping existing services and detail specific improvements they believe are needed. More in-depth studies will be conducted as projects are selected.

Key informants are identified by an organizational steering committee assembled by the initial group of persons seeking action on a community problem or problems. In developing this initial list of key informants, the steering committee will want to include participants from all major social and economic groups. For example, key informants could include knowledgeable persons from community education and service organizations, advocacy groups, political leaders, faith-based organizations, business leaders, etc. This would include leaders in organizations that perform the following community functions:

- Economic (e.g., businesses and labor unions)
- Mutual Assistance (e.g., "natural" support networks and social agencies)
- Social Participation (e.g., churches and civic organizations)
- Social Integration (e.g., chambers of commerce and neighborhood associations)
- Social Control (e.g., law enforcement)

The steering committee will want to limit survey participation to those who have expressed interest in, or are likely to initiate action to improve health and income security outcomes.

The survey should be conducted in person by a steering committee member (possibly the steering committee member who recommended the participant) and the staff organizer. The survey will consist of open-ended questions such as:

- What are this community's strengths and assets in providing residents with health and economic security resources?
- What are the weaknesses and barriers to making progress on these needs?
- Who else do we need to involve if we are to be successful?
- Are you willing to help?

As noted above, the survey can be utilized to identify potential members for a coalition by the inclusion of a reputational question. For example, "Who would you want on your team if you wanted to get something done in this community?"

The number of persons to be interviewed will depend on many factors, including the size of the community, the number of organizations, and community networks. Starting with a small number of participants (approximately twenty-five) may be desirable to assess the process and information being collected and make adjustments where needed. It's important to note that the list of interviewees almost always grows as interviews are completed and potential new key informants are identified.

Be sure to schedule interviews in advance. Enough time should be allowed for the participants to feel comfortable answering questions fully; I recommend a minimum of forty-five minutes. An essential function of the interview is to enable the participant to connect with members of the organi-zation and participate in the planning process. Additional interviews may be conducted to fill information gaps and ensure all key groups are included.

STEP 2: DEVELOPING TENTATIVE RECOMMENDATIONS FOR ACTION

After completing the survey, the steering committee—assisted by the organizer—will tabulate findings from the interview. Tentative recommendations for action will be developed. These include:

- Listing and ranking priority needs identified by participants
- Identifying potential leaders to involve in future organizational activities
- Identifying possible short- and long-term goals
- Suggesting next steps in organization building and goal setting

STEP 3: COMMUNITY MEETING(S)

All participants in the key informant survey should be invited to a community meeting by the organizational steering committee. At the meeting, survey participants will receive a report of survey findings and be asked for feedback. In particular, the steering committee will want to know if the participants feel that the community needs, priorities, and proposed goals are accurate and if additions or deletions are necessary. It's also important to request feedback on additional persons to involve in the planning process. Key informant survey participants may decide to meet subsequently to get updates on progress.

4

SELECT INFORMANTS

First, identify the groups and categories of organizations from which key informants should be drawn. Diverse interests and perceptions should be captured. Set an initial limit on the number of interviewees.

5

TAKE NOTES

Take detailed notes on answers to each interview question.

 **6**

ANALYZE RESULTS

Analyze the interview data and present the findings to leadership, partners, and survey participants.

Participants should also be given the opportunity to volunteer to assist with specific action steps. Following the meeting, the steering committee should review and modify initial recommendations as appropriate in response to feedback. The steering committee can then move to develop a more formal organizational structure and an initial set of goals and objectives.

SETTING GOALS

IMPORTANCE OF GOAL STATEMENTS

Well-stated goals make many contributions to an organization's success:

- Make clear to members, potential members, partners, and funders what the organization seeks to accomplish
- Provide both a focus and limits to alternative approaches to improve outcomes
- In times of significant challenges, they remind members of the importance of the shared aspirations that led them to establish the organization and, thus, are a source of renewed energy to achieve those aspirations

CHARACTERISTICS OF GOAL STATEMENTS

Good goal statements should:

- Clarify and narrow the organization's focus without unnecessarily eliminating options for achieving them
- Express "ideal" conditions to be achieved
- Not provide specific time frames for achieving progress on outcomes (This is a function and objective discussed below.)

The Problem-Solving Process described in Chapter III discusses the selection of time-limited and qualified objectives for each goal.

EXAMPLE: GOAL STATEMENT ON PUBLIC TRANSPORTATION

To ensure that all City of Enid, Oklahoma residents have access to safe and affordable transportation for employment, education, shopping, health, and other community services.

Note that this goal statement does not limit the mode of transportation (e.g., bus, shared ride taxi, or rail), specific hours of operation for initial services, or time frame for completion of the goal. These specifics are subsequently covered in the Statement of Objectives.

INITIAL ORGANIZATIONAL GOALS

The key informant survey discussed previously secures input from community leaders on priority needs of the community, assets (e.g., leaders, organizations, and financial resources), and possible alternatives for meeting needs. Tabulation of survey findings will provide information on the number of respondents who see specific needs as a priority. As part of the goal-setting process, the organizational steering committee may want to compare this information with other recent community surveys, health status reports from local and state organizations, and additional relevant information. The steering committee should then develop recommendations for action, including goal statements to present at the survey respondents' meeting discussed in the previous section. Taking this feedback into account, the steering committee will be ready to finalize initial goals for the organization.

DECIDING ON INITIAL SCOPE AND PRIORITIES FOR THE GOAL STATEMENT

In selecting the number of goals and priorities for action, the steering committee should consider the following questions:

- Which goals were most frequently seen as priorities by survey respondents?
- For which of the priority needs and goals identified by the survey were the most respondents willing to be a part of organized action?
- Which specific goals identified through the survey will the organization need to combine to secure broad community support?
- Given the challenges, should the organization take on a significant but achievable short-term goal and a more challenging goal for long-term action?

A MODEL FOR COMMUNITY EMPOWERMENT TO IMPROVE LOCAL HEALTH, EDUCATION, AND INCOME SECURITY OUTCOMES

Goal Setting: Community Case Example

As a new organization, The Community Development Support Association (CDSA) of Enid, Oklahoma, experienced the goal-setting challenges discussed above in its start-up phase.

Participants in its key informant survey identified public transportation as a high-priority community need. The YWCA had conducted a community survey documenting its need for public transportation and had persistently pressed the Enid City Council to take positive action. City officials, however, initially discounted the information and refused to act. CDSA steering committee members, which included YWCA leaders, gave transportation priority ranking for immediate action. Health care for low-income families and affordable housing were also priorities. At the time, though, affordable housing was a need that the organization's financial and political resources seemed insufficient to take on.

Further, no one among the survey respondents indicated an interest in leading a housing initiative. Some steering committee members felt that the feasibility of securing financing for health care expansion was unlikely. However, two committee members had ideas about actions the organization could take to redirect and expand the use of existing resources. The lead nurse at Oklahoma University's Family Medical Clinic believed there was a way to greatly increase utilization of early periodic screening and diagnostic testing program funds available through Medicaid to help families secure medical homes and specialized medical services. Another steering committee member stated that CDSA should take action to ensure the Enid area secured a Community Mental Health Center. Funding was available, but an application had not been submitted, and, at the time, the organization that had accepted the responsibility to write the grant was not making progress.

With this information, the steering committee decided to adopt all three goals as there was substantial support for each goal among the survey participants. The Committee chose to take priority action on transportation, expanding health care to low-income families, and securing a community mental health center since it had commitments from steering committee members and survey participants to take an active role in achieving these goals.

Expanding the supply of quality affordable housing was established as a long-term goal. As noted in subsequent detailed case studies, these goal-setting decisions led to significant accomplishments in all four goal areas.

CHAPTER IV

Building an Organization

RECRUITING LEADERSHIP AND SUSTAINING INVOLVEMENT

Building an organization that helps empower a community to achieve priority goals can be both an exciting and challenging experience for participants. Over the years, I have found that local leaders are frequently encouraged that "someone is finally going to do something about a problem."

At the same time, potential participants, based on previous negative experiences, may be skeptical that the new organization can—or will—be successful. Even so, many leaders are eager to help when presented with a plan that shows potential for improving local conditions.

Building an organization that helps empower a community to achieve priority goals can be both an exciting and challenging experience for participants.

CASE STUDY #3
Identifying Leaders for the Community Development Support Association

The following example presents critical aspects of leadership recruitment and retention in a community organization.

During the development of the Community Development Support Association (CDSA) in Enid, Oklahoma, I was responsible for conducting a key informant survey. As part of the survey, I interviewed a woman who was an active community leader holding important roles in the YWCA, United Way, and other organizations. She had recently run for mayor and, unfortunately, lost. The Enid YWCA operated a robust domestic violence program and had long advocated for the development of public transportation in Enid. As part of its advocacy, the YWCA completed a survey documenting the need for public transportation services. The YWCA had approached the City of Enid with persistent requests for action on transportation without success. Despite the survey findings, the City's response was to deny the request. Throughout the interview, given her recent experiences, this leader was somewhat doubtful about the possibility that our new organization could bring about needed change. At the same time, I felt that her passion for community improvement and her experience, wisdom, and linkages to key leaders and organizations could help enact change. Further, the new organization could help to achieve some of her long-held aspirations.

Near the end of the interview, after giving the leader details of our plans, I asked her if she would be willing to serve on the CDSA Steering Committee. She said something about being very disappointed about the community's inaction on major problems, paused momentarily, and then said, "I like what you are saying; I doubt that it will work, but I'm willing to help." I was thrilled by her response, knowing full well that we were both taking a risk. She once again trusted that citizen action could achieve real change. Knowing her recent disappointments and the great value of her trust, I did not want to disappoint her.

This leader joined the CDSA Steering Committee and, subsequently, the organization's Board of Directors. Her leadership, the leadership of the other Board members, and finally, the leadership from the City of Enid resulted in the establishment of a public transportation system. Over the years, she provided excellent leadership as Chairman of the Board. She also served in committee roles and led projects to improve housing, early childhood development, school success, and juvenile services.

My experiences with the CDSA and dozens of experiences before and after have reinforced my belief that it is vital for community planning and action Boards of Directors to focus on recruiting volunteer leaders that help build the combined competencies required for achieving positive change. This is mainly the responsibility of the Board of Directors, and it's nominating committee.

EFFECTIVE MEETINGS

Well-run meetings are at the heart of planning and action and significantly impact an organization's success in improving community outcomes. Effective meetings are vital for recruiting and sustaining the participation of members, partners, and supporters in every step of the problem-solving process. This includes internal organizational meetings of the membership body, Board, committees, partners, and consultants; it also includes external meetings with public and private organizations to seek changes in policy, programs, and funding. The quality of meetings can significantly impact the achievement of organizational objectives.

Effective meetings are vital for recruiting and sustaining participation of members, partners, and supporters.

The following comparison of possible consequences of "well-run" and "poorly-run" meetings is focused primarily on Board and committee meetings. It also includes principles to consider for the full range of organizational meetings.

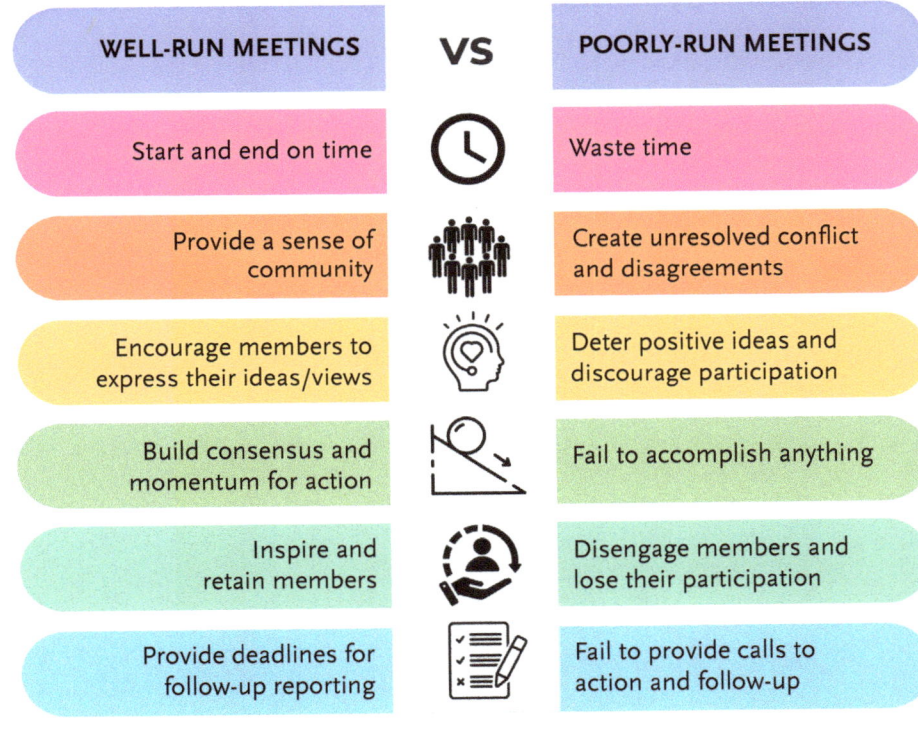

WELL-RUN MEETINGS	VS	POORLY-RUN MEETINGS
Start and end on time		Waste time
Provide a sense of community		Create unresolved conflict and disagreements
Encourage members to express their ideas/views		Deter positive ideas and discourage participation
Build consensus and momentum for action		Fail to accomplish anything
Inspire and retain members		Disengage members and lose their participation
Provide deadlines for follow-up reporting		Fail to provide calls to action and follow-up

AGENDAS

Agendas are an essential tool for expediting goal achievement through meetings. A good agenda can:

- Give the chairperson a mechanism for keeping the group focused on tasks
- Recognize the leadership roles of members
- Encourage broad participation in decision-making
- Clarify volunteer and staff roles
- Help facilitate follow-up on group decisions

The following is a proposed basic template and guide for Board and committee meetings. The agenda is focused on encouraging inclusive

```
+--------------------------------------------------------------------------+
|                          MEETING AGENDA                                  |
|                  Planning and Action Organization                        |
|                        Board of Directors                                |
|                      Jane Bell, Chairperson                              |
+--------------------------------------------------------------------------+
```

MEETING AGENDA
Planning and Action Organization
Board of Directors
Jane Bell, Chairperson

Meeting date: Monday, February 22, 2021
Start time: 9:00 a.m.   End time: 10:30 a.m.
Meeting location: Enid City Hall, 401 W Owen K Garriott Rd, Enid, OK 73701

TIME	Description	Presenter
9:00 a.m.	Call to Order and Introductions	Jane Bell, Chairperson
9:10 a.m.	Review and Action — December Meeting Minutes	Jane Bell
9:15 a.m.	Progress in Establishing Transit Authority	Ray Glynn, Transportation Committee Chair
9:25 a.m.	Recommendations for Parents As Teachers Fund Committee — Discussion and Possible Action	Renee Walker, Committee Chair
9:50 a.m.	Need for Low-Income Housing — Discussion and Possible Action	Ellen Frazer
10:10 a.m.	Finance Committee Report — Discussion	Joe Edwards, Finance Committee Chair
10:20 a.m.	Next Steps — Assignments and Next Meeting Date	Jane Bell
10:30 a.m.	Meeting adjourned	Jane Bell

February Meeting   page 1 of 1

participation in decision-making and advancing the organization's progress toward objectives. Each meeting should include:

- Review and action of minutes from the previous meeting
- Feedback on successes and failures in carrying out previous decisions
- At least one decision in an area vital to the organization's objectives
- Brainstorming on new issues (where appropriate)
- Finance reports
- Next steps and who is responsible

PRE-MEETING PREPARATION—A VITAL INVESTMENT

Professional staff members carry out a wide range of responsibilities between meetings to help ensure productive meetings (as well as strengthen the organization's political, economic, and program capacities.) Responsibilities include meeting with the Board chair and other members on agenda and priority issues, research, preparation of proposals, written communications with members, preparing and mailing/emailing meeting announcements and minutes, etc.

Professional staff responsibilities include:

A. Meeting with the chairman and other leaders prior to the meeting.
- Chairman
    - Review and post the agenda
    - Discuss decisions needed and possible conflicts
    - Next steps in the implementation of coalition decisions
- Other Leaders (such as committee chairpersons)
    - Prepare and review reports to be made and action needed

B. Spending time with other board members to:
- Learn about their personal objectives for participation in the board, positions on issues, and additional issues they feel the group should address
- Help build organizational consensus leading to positive action on objectives. This may include learning of dissent on issues that must be dealt with if the board is to make wise choices.

C. Preparation of the Physical Meeting Environment
- Environmental factors can make it impossible for a group to conduct business successfully. Distractions such as noise, phone calls, excessive heat or cold, or lack of privacy may prevent focus on complex issues.
- The room for a meeting should provide a safe, comfortable, well-lighted, "upbeat" space for work. Further, the location of the meetings can communicate symbolically the nature and significance of the group's work. For example, a meeting in the City Manager's conference room could help communicate that the group is working on a project of major public importance. Food or refreshments may contribute to

member enjoyment and group participation while recognizing that some volunteers may have had to miss a meal or forgo a break to participate. The room's physical layout should facilitate interaction and provide material and equipment for reports, discussions, video presentations, etc. To save time, equipment should be in place prior to the meetings.

D. Preparation of Reports and Documentation

- If committees have been appointed to study and make recommendations to the total group, professional staff should make sure these groups meet and are prepared to report at the next meeting. The staff should meet with subgroups and, where appropriate, prepare a written report for use by the committee chairperson.

E. Mailings/Emails to Members Before the Meeting and Encouraging Participation

- In most instances, professional staff persons(s) should prepare minutes of coalition meetings. These should be mailed/emailed about one week before the meetings, along with an agenda for the meeting and any proposals that will require action. Members should be contacted before meetings to encourage participation. Broad participation is critical in avoiding repetitive meetings and to get proper involvement in organizational choices and actions.

MEETING MINUTES

In most instances, minutes should be brief and to the point. Minutes should include:

- Decisions along with makers and seconds of motions
- Credit for member contributions in decision-making
- Brief highlights of committee reports
- Implementation responsibilities accepted by members and staff, along with dates and time frames

Brief minutes that capture important courses of action and members' contributions are more likely to be read. This also helps limit excessive time spent in preparation and review of minutes.

MEETING LEADERSHIP

At least two critical types of leadership are vital in strengthening task groups: task leadership and social-emotional leadership.

Task Leadership

- Leaders keep the group focused on its objectives for a meeting, bringing the discussion back to the favorable resolution of the problem at hand. Leaders may also propose policies that take into account complex issues and diverse points of view. They ensure that individual members with vital information needed for decision-making are encouraged to speak. They follow up to make sure group decisions are implemented.

Social and Emotional Leadership

- This type of leadership helps individual members fulfill their needs for social participation through the group. These needs range from participating in a problem-solving process to participating in a support system. Personal recognition, conflict resolution, and personal growth through assertive expression are further examples of needs that may be fulfilled through the group process. If the group is responsive to individual members' social and emotional needs, retention is enhanced.

SECURING AND SUSTAINING PARTICIPATION

The following is a discussion of additional organizational characteristics that can contribute to success in recruiting and sustaining participation.

NOMINATING COMMITTEE

- A nominating committee whose membership includes linkages to diverse populations the organization works to engage can contribute greatly to the organization's success. The Nominating Committee can recommend persons for board and committee membership to fill critical roles in assessing needs, developing alternative solutions, and influencing decision-making.

- Participants need precise definitions of the roles they are asked to fill and possible contributions they may be able to make in achieving organizational objectives. Participants must also know what support they can expect from executive leadership and staff.

- There should be opportunities for new participants to test the fit of their organizational responsibilities within their time availability and aspirations. A time-limited acceptance of duties is one option for gaining vital involvement.
- A supportive organizational environment that responds to participant feedback on organizational actions and participants' roles is conducive to participant retention.

BUILDING AN ORGANIZATIONAL STRUCTURE

Central to the planning and action organization's success is creating and operating a sound organizational structure. Both volunteers and staff need—and expect—clarity and support in their roles and responsibilities. This allows both to understand and depend on organizational expectations. As noted previously, failure to provide clarity can lead to a sense of powerlessness, organizational failure, and loss of participants (Freeman, 1972). Planning and action organizations frequently deal with high levels of complexity in assessing needs, developing effective technical and political strategies, and implementing change. This can be overwhelming to volunteers and staff alike. For example, a Board meeting can get 'bogged down' in dealing with too many details surrounding a complex issue, leading to frustration and despair. Referring the matter to a specialized committee can provide the time and technical skills needed. The committee can then make a report with recommendations to the Board. Sometimes, the Board may need to change organizational structure to address problems (such as adding member committees/consultants or partnerships, etc.). The organization's bylaws provide a means for making these changes.

Organization Bylaws

The organization's bylaws spell out both the organization's mission and its structure to accomplish the mission. If local planning and action organizations are to be both inclusive and influential in community decision-making, the organization needs to provide a variety of avenues for local citizens to participate and provide support. See the Appendix for a nonprofit bylaws example.

Note: Consider meeting with an attorney who understands nonprofit law if your organization receives public funds. Bylaw requirements vary from state to state. Also, be wary of bylaws that become so complicated that they are rarely read or used. Remember to keep bylaws that communicate as clearly and simply as possible.

ORGANIZATIONAL STRUCTURE COMPONENTS

The following is a detailed discussion of critical structure elements for community planning and action organizations, providing various avenues for local participation.

Membership Body

The Membership Body can provide opportunities for participation by persons who support the organization, including Board and committee members, but also a broad range of persons who serve in neither of these roles. Membership groups can be open-ended because of their limited number of meetings and functions. Yet, these groups can significantly strengthen the organization's capacity as an influential coalition, its linkages to residents and partner organizations, and the quality of participation afforded to members.

Typically, membership groups meet once or twice a year and perform the following functions:

- Hear brief annual reports of projects, achievements, and finances
- Hold an annual fundraiser
- Elect Board members and officers

Board and Directors

Boards and Directors provide governance for the organization on the full range of programs, policies, financing, personnel, and other issues. Mission-centered and effective governance by the organization's Board of Directors is essential for initial and sustained success. Selection and sustaining participation of Board members who are passionate about the organization's mission and prioritize the mission above other interests is vital in improving local outcomes and maintaining community trust and support of the organization. Detailed discussion of the Board's role is illustrated in the bylaws example provided in the Appendix.

Volunteer Leadership

Throughout my career, I have been greatly inspired by volunteer leaders' dedication, determination, and contributions to the development of local support systems and opportunities that lead to improved outcomes for local populations. Further, these leaders have helped build democratic norms in the community, not only by modeling democratic behavior, but also by demonstrating the great possibilities and benefits of effective local action for change. The assets that volunteer-driven planning and action organizations can bring to improve local well-being have been discussed in previous chapters and illustrated in case examples throughout the book. For this section, two vital characteristics are highlighted.

1. Commitment to Inclusiveness

Community planning and action organizations must embody the principles they encourage their communities to follow in decision-making. Therefore, these organizations need leaders committed to and effective in securing, sustaining, and supporting the active participation of major populations to be served, as well as leadership from the broader community.

2. Commitment to Action

Disaffection with organizations too often has resulted from volunteer experiences of "all talk but no significant action." Sometimes, organizations do an excellent job of "selling the problem" as a means of securing financial and volunteer support rather than acting to put evidenced-based solutions in place.

Influential leaders demonstrate a persistent commitment to the achievement of improved conditions. Successful volunteer leaders are willing to "go the distance" and support members when the barriers seem insurmountable. They also recognize the need to celebrate milestones toward achieving objectives.

Professional Staff Support

While local planning and action organizations are volunteer-driven, and volunteer leaders are active in both the planning and implementation of objectives, providing skilled professional staff support is an essential element for the success of community planning and action organizations. Detailed discussion of staff roles and responsibilities are covered in this chapter and Chapter VII. The roles of volunteer leaders and professional staff and the complementary nature of these roles is provided in Chapter V and Chapter IV.

Partners

Partnerships with other organizations with common goals and complementary relationships can benefit the partners and the community as a whole. Examples of two types of partnerships are discussed below. In the examples, the Community Development Support Association entered into two types of partnerships to establish a community-wide school health program. It's important to note that these are only two of many possibilities.

Partners Who Operate New and Innovative Programs

As described in Chapter III, a CDSA survey identified a priority need for health services for low-income families. Enid Public Schools had identified the need for mental health services but lacked funding. The schools could easily integrate mental health services with their existing school counseling program, which was primarily focused on academic counseling. In discussions with the Regional Director of the Federal Early Periodic Screening and Diagnostic Testing (EPSDT) program, the organization learned that EPSDT funds could be used for mental health screening and follow-up services. CDSA partnered with Enid Public Schools to deliver mental health services through a contract with the District Office of EPSDT. CDSA's partnership with the regional office included facilitating the relationship with Enid Public Schools and forming a partnership oversight committee that met regularly to hear reports on program implementation and make changes needed for desired outcomes. Further, CDSA was also in partnership with the Garfield County Department of Human Services, Garfield County Health Department, and Family Medicine Clinic to increase EPSDT utilization by families served by the agency.

CONSULTANTS

Consultants (whether paid or volunteer) can help round out an organization's technical and/or political capacity by filling in knowledge and skill gaps and expanding professional hours available to work on a specialized need. Volunteer consultation can come through relationships with partner organizations or individuals with specialized knowledge serving on committees or boards. Paid consultants can also help with specialized financial, political, and technical needs. They can help solve a specific problem (such as selecting modes of transportation for a city) or assist with internal organizational needs.

CASE STUDY #4
The Benefits of Consultants

The following is an example of consultation the Community Development Support Association (CDSA) planning and action organization volunteers provided.

As noted earlier, CDSA (through its key informant survey) identified health care for low-income families as a priority; CDSA formed a health committee to explore alternative approaches to accomplish this goal and to make recommendations for action to the Board. Two of the members of the Committee were the Director of the Oklahoma Community Family Practice Clinic in Enid, Oklahoma and the head nurse for the clinic. Both of these members were dedicated to improving health care for low-income families. The clinic Director was also active in the Oklahoma State Medical Association and an editor of their journal. The head nurse was passionate about the need and was also a member of the CDSA Board.

As the Committee was experiencing serious challenges in finding resources to expand health, these two members drew upon their direct experience with low-income families and their knowledge of Medicaid funding. Their volunteer consultation provided active participation in the Health Committee and Board, which proved invaluable and improved health care access for children in Enid.

Several important findings included:

- Many low-income families used hospital emergency services as their primary form of health care

- Emergency room care is costly and sporadic and does not provide patients with continuity of care provided in a medical home

- The Early Periodic Screening and Diagnostic Testing program could provide testing and medical services and function as a medical home for children. However, the program had low usage (perhaps 10%) due to several factors (e.g., families' lack of knowledge about benefits, failure to keep medical enrollment updated, lack of transportation, and the limited numbers of doctors accepting Medicaid)

CHAPTER V

Using a Problem-Solving Process to Guide Technical and Political Action

Chronic failure of a community to deal with significant issues frequently leads to extreme frustration, apathy, and despair. Therefore, when approaching an organization about a problem, it may respond, "We just don't have the resources," or "We need a transportation system, but the city power structure is not about to budge." In some instances, the responses are based on recent experiences in which volunteer leaders have put substantial energy into an effort only to be rebuffed by decision-makers. In other cases, a long history of inaction produces a sense of powerlessness, resulting in negative attitudes and norms.

There are also factors relating to the difficulty of change, which can lead communities to resist action. Significant change can take massive amounts of time and energy. Opponents may have positions and resources that put them at a great advantage. Also, solutions may be complex and require the cooperation of many individuals and entities. Finally, change may require broad community support, and some leaders may wonder if this support can be secured. A scientifically grounded approach can make it possible for planning and action organizations to:

- Assist volunteer leaders, staff, and partners find roles that make effective use of their knowledge, skills, financial support, and time
- Integrate and focus multiple community assets (e.g., inclusive participation, leadership, technical resources, and political resources) in productive ways to achieve outcomes
- Prevent dead-ends based on poorly researched solutions
- Avoid unnecessary disappointment and hopelessness about the possibility of meaningful change

The following illustration shows the steps in the problem-solving process and the associated roles of volunteers, members of the Board, organization members, and staff members.

We covered the first two steps in the problem-solving process: Problem Identification and Goal Setting and Inclusive Engagement of Local Leaders in Building an Organization in Chapter III. This chapter focuses on Problem Analysis and Developing and Selecting Alternatives.

An effective problem-solving process can address these challenges and help bring small victories, increased energy, and support, followed by even greater achievements.

Volunteer and Professional Roles in the Community Problem-Solving Process

STEPS	VOLUNTEER ROLES	PROFESSIONAL ROLES
Problem identification	Voice discontent; link with community constituencies; decide which problems to pursue	Secure existing data on scope and nature of problem; conduct surveys; facilitate group process
Organization building	Identify members who can fill positions requiring consumer input, influence, and technical expertise; select members	Suggest structures and processes to solve problems; help members find and fulfill productive roles in organization
Problem analysis and established objectives	Each member brings expertise in political, technical, and/or consumer areas; review technical data supplied by staff	Use research and analytic tools to help group analyze problem; establish objectives and means for achieving them
Develop alternatives	Suggest alternatives; weigh information presented by staff and other members	Based on input from group and technical information, develop succinct well-stated alternatives and present them in written form
Select alternatives	Make decisions	Present recommendations
Implementation	Conduct political work in implementation	Manage organizational initiative to implement decisions
Feedback and program modification	Review data on program results; decide program modifications	Conduct research on program outcomes, or secure evaluation research from outside sources

PROBLEM ANALYSIS

I made extensive use of the systems model in analyzing decision-making as part of my doctoral dissertation. The dissertation examined educational policy-making at the state level in West Virginia. I found the model tremendously helpful in understanding what led to important changes in state-level decisions impacting public education. Subsequently, I found the model useful for analyzing existing decision-making systems, problem analysis, and strategic planning to achieve vital changes in policy and outcomes. A detailed discussion of the systems model and case examples, which illustrate a variety of uses for the model, are provided in Chapters V and VI. The systems model is an excellent analytic tool for planning and action organizations to use in all aspects of the problem-solving process. It can be helpful in:

- Providing a visual illustration of the system currently in place, which is helpful in pinpointing weaknesses in the current system and/or identifying how it maintains adverse conditions
- Identifying alternative points of intervention that could improve outcomes
- Weighing which alternatives could fit the local planning and action organization's current or potential political and technical resources for achieving objectives
- Selecting appropriate technical and political alternatives
- Establishing achievable objectives

The following diagram illustrates system operations. The system could be a group, an organization, or a group of organizations collaborating to achieve a common goal.

System components include inputs, sub-systems, outputs, feedback, and boundaries.

Basic Systems Model

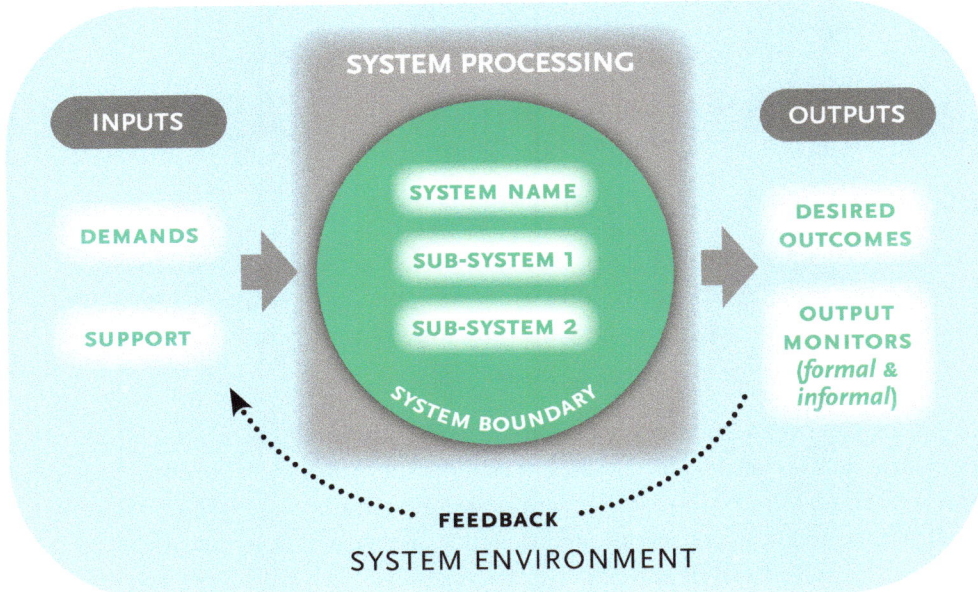

USING A PROBLEM-SOLVING PROCESS TO GUIDE TECHNICAL AND POLITICAL ACTION

Local Public School System Example

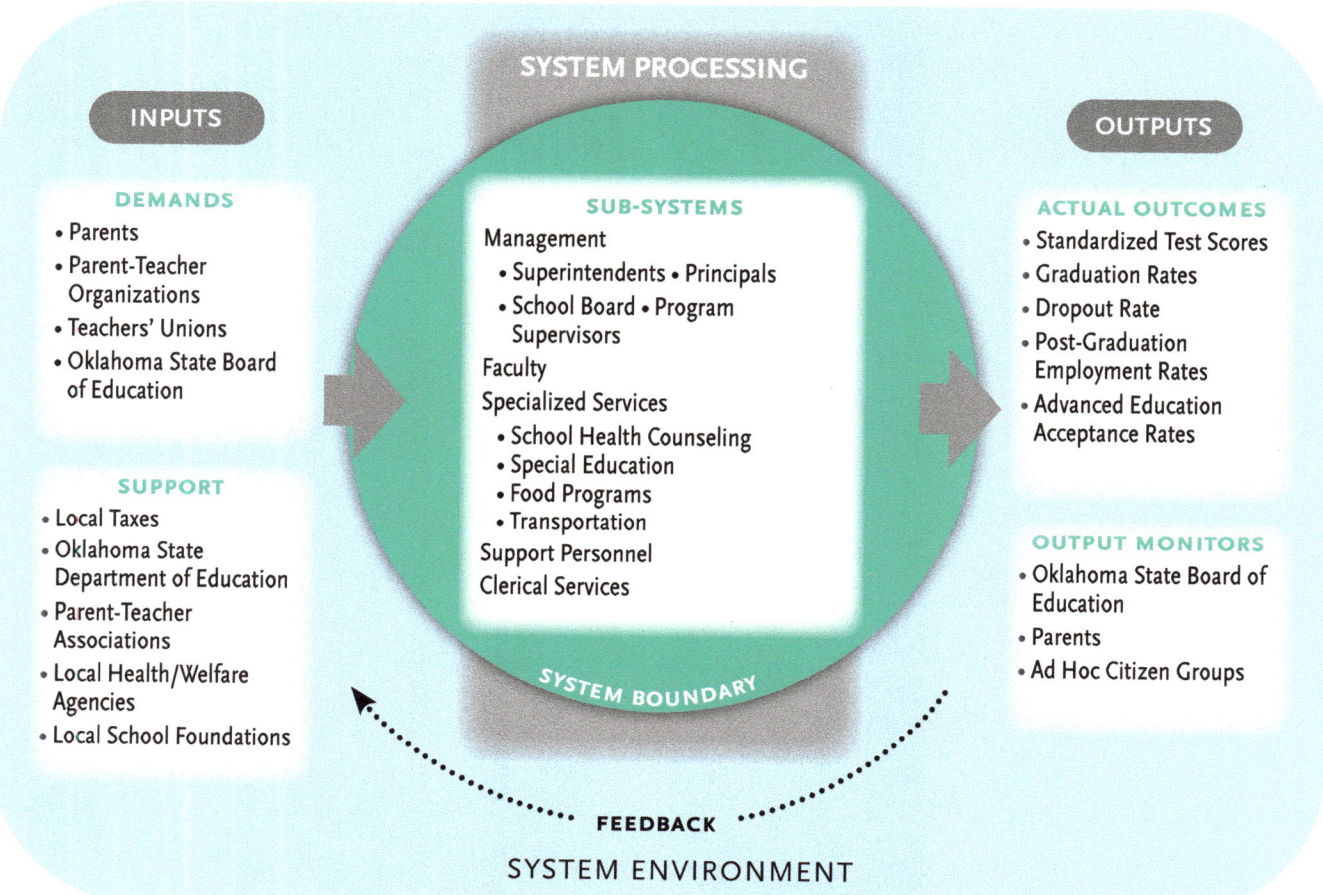

DISCUSSION OF THE SYSTEM MODEL

System components include inputs, sub-systems, outputs, feedback, and boundaries. The diagram above illustrates the application of the model as it could be used to help analyze an existing public school system.

INPUTS

Inputs can come in the form of demands and support. Demands might come from individual parents, parent-teacher organizations, teachers' unions, the State Board of Education, or the local health department. Support might come from local taxes, the State Department of Education, parent-teacher associations, partnerships with local health and welfare agencies, or local school foundations.

SUB-SYSTEMS

Sub-systems perform specific processing functions for organizations. The processing functions are aimed at producing desired outcomes. Sub-systems might include management (e.g., superintendents, principals, school board, and program supervisors), faculty, specialized services (e.g., school health, counseling, special education, food programs, and transportation), support personnel, and clerical services.

OUTPUTS

Outputs are the actual outcomes achieved from the system processing inputs. In this instance, outputs could include standardized student scores, graduation rates, dropout rates, and student success in moving into employment or advanced education.

OUTPUT MONITORS

Formal monitors would include the State Board of Education. Informal monitors could include parents and ad hoc citizen groups.

FEEDBACK

Feedback from the environment may translate into demands and/or support for the system. Feedback can come from the State Board of Education on school success in meeting standards, local parent-teacher associations, school unions on issues such as salary and teaching conditions, and local employers on graduate preparedness for entry-level employment.

BOUNDARIES

Boundaries function to separate the system from the larger environment. Entities included in the system directly perform some function for the system. For example, while individual state legislators have a role in funding decisions for the school, they have no direct authority within the school system.

USING THE PROBLEM-SOLVING PROCESS: DEVELOPING AND SELECTING ALTERNATIVES

As a local planning and action organization moves from analyzing problems to developing alternative solutions that will lead to improved outcomes, the organization faces the challenge of creating workable courses of action. This can be one of the most exciting and/or frustrating experiences for participants. Alternatives for both technical and political requirements may be needed.

On the technical side, numerous questions need to be answered, including:

- What evidence-based policies and programs have been utilized to address this need?
- What requirement for innovation will the community need to meet?
- Will new opportunities be relevant, accessible, and acceptable to the populations being served?
- Does the community have the organizational capacity to deliver the proposed programs with fidelity?

On the political side are questions including:

- What are the resources and requirements for proposed policies and programs? Are potential sources available?
- What decision-making systems must be influenced to secure resources, changes in policy, and changes in delivery systems?
- What political resources and strategies does the planning and action organization need to influence decision-making?

Establishing Objectives

Establishing measurable objectives is an essential ingredient in a sound problem-solving process. As we noted earlier in the discussion of goal statements, goals are broad, ideal statements of conditions to be achieved. Objectives are specific, measurable statements of progress toward goals to be achieved within a specific time frame. An organization may choose to pursue multiple objectives toward a single goal. These highly specific objective statements:

- Provide a focus for organizational responses and guidance for the Board and staff
- Provide for measurement of success and encourage timely adjustments in approach if actions are not accomplished
- Provide evidence of organizational effectiveness to consumers, partners, and funders
- Make clear the possible limits of goal achievements within a specific time frame to avoid over promising and resulting disappointment to potential program participants, organization members, partners, and funders

Establishing measurable objectives is an essential ingredient in a sound problem-solving process.

Example of a Statement of Objective

The Step Up Program will have funding, staffing, and partnership relationships to begin a pilot program offering assistance to homeless youth starting October 1, 2020. This program will assist youth in securing housing, education, employment, and transportation based on the specific needs of each participant. Initially, the program will be able to serve five youths at any one time.

CASE STUDY #5

The Problem-Solving Process

The following is a community case example where the local planning and action organization used the problem-solving process. This process helped move a community from a situation that initially seemed somewhat "hopeless" to significantly improving local outcomes and the ability to share innovations with communities facing similar challenges.

In the early stage of the Community Development Support Association's (CDSA's) development, a key informant survey was conducted to help identify priority community needs. Lack of health care for low-income children and families was broadly considered a priority for action. CDSA appointed a Health Care Committee to study the need and develop recommendations for action by the Board of Directors. When CDSA announced that it was forming a Committee to provide leadership for action on child health care, there was considerable interest in participation. Persons expressing interest included the lead nurse and physician manager of the local University of Oklahoma's (OU) Family Practice Clinic, a Neighborhood Association leader, the Director of the Garfield County Health Department, a private physician, and a local attorney. These individuals were ultimately appointed to CDSA's Health Committee.

The Committee began a detailed study of the problem and possible solutions. In addition to data from the key informant survey, the Committee reviewed data on health indicators from the Oklahoma State Department of Health. The direct patient experience of the OU physician, lead nurse, and Health Department staff was beneficial, as was consumer information provided by the neighborhood association leader. Committee members pointed out that numerous families relied on hospital emergency rooms for health care and frequently visited emergency rooms only after serious problems had developed. For many families, preventive health care and a continuum of care from a primary care physician were nonexistent.

In exploring financial resources, the Committee learned that, due to the high cost of health care, United Way resources were probably not an option for dealing with the scope of existing needs. There was general agreement that Medicaid expansion at that time was not probable. However, the lead nurse with the OU Family Practice Clinic pointed out that the Early and Periodic Screening, Diagnostic, and Treatment (EOSDT) component of Medicaid was poorly utilized (about 10% of eligible families in the County were accessing these services at that time.)

This program was a vital resource as it provided:

- Children with regular periodic visits (beginning at birth) with a primary care physician for screenings

- Treatment for problems identified through the screenings

- Potential for establishing medical homes for participants

The EPSDT program was administered locally through the County Department of Human Services office. The CDSA Health Committee invited the program supervisor to be a member of the Committee. When asked about the low utilization rates of EPSDT, the supervisor said the families had little interest in the program and frequently allowed their Medicaid eligibility to lapse, thus losing access to EPSDT.

USING THE SYSTEMS MODELS TO HELP IDENTIFY ALTERNATIVES AND SET OBJECTIVES

The CDSA Health Committee realized that there was great promise for improving the health of Medicaid participants' children. However, current barriers were negating those possibilities. The systems model provided a helpful tool for addressing alternative strategies for change. This case study demonstrates the *evolution* of the Child Health Care System to achieve improved opportunities and outcomes.

The following systems diagram illustrates major elements of the local health care system serving children of low-income families at the beginning of the CDSA initiatives. Each system component will be discussed, including input (demands and support), processing (aimed at achieving desired outcomes) by major sub-systems, outcomes (desired and actual), and feedback (monitors and content feedback).

INPUTS

Phase 1: Child Health Care System *Before* CDSA Initiative:
Using the System's Model to Identify and Analyze the Problem, Alternatives, Solutions, and Set Objectives

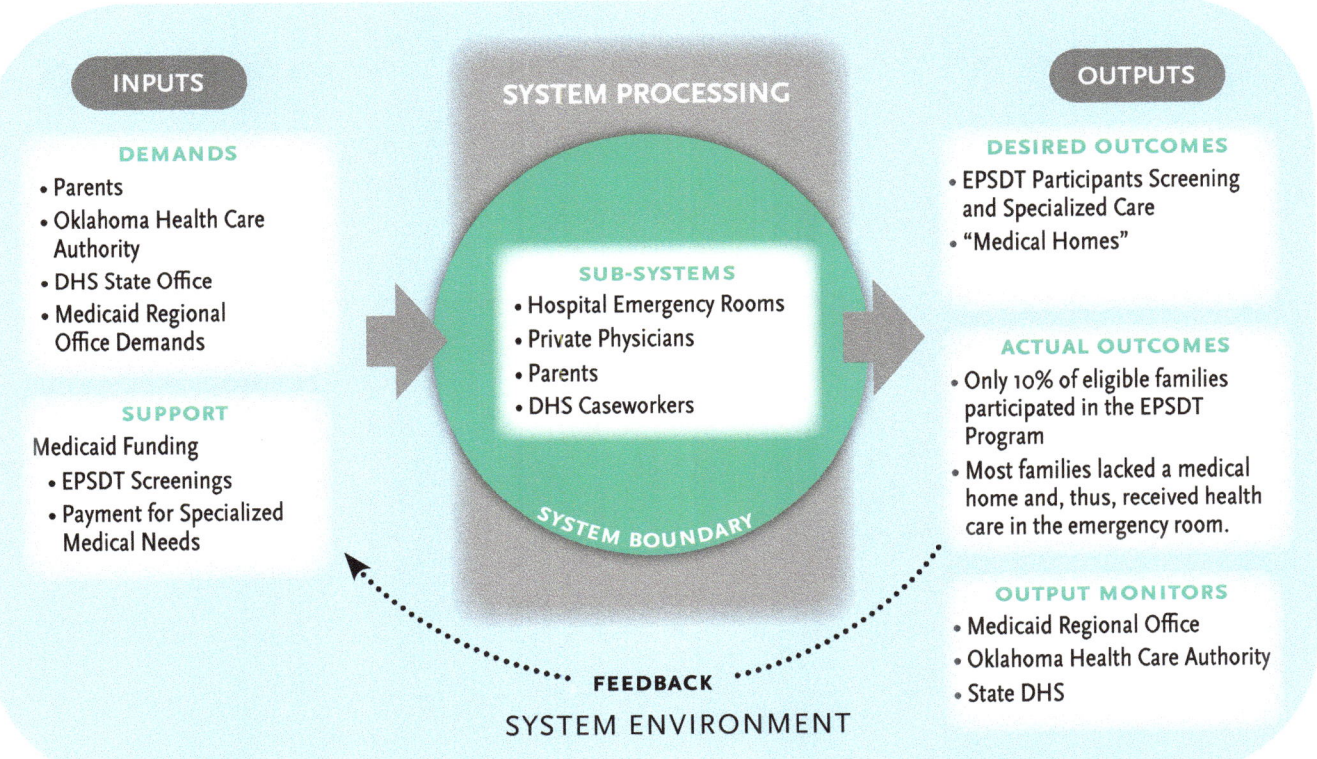

Demands

- The Regional Medicaid office monitors state-level achievement of standards

- Parents seek health care for children, but only 10% participate in EPSDT. Most families secure care in emergency rooms

- Oklahoma Health Care Authority monitors the program and encourages full use of EPSDT

- The Oklahoma State Department of Human Services (DHS) monitors county offices

USING A PROBLEM-SOLVING PROCESS TO GUIDE TECHNICAL AND POLITICAL ACTION

Support

Medicaid provides funding for all Medicaid families to receive:

- EDPDT screenings
- Specialized medical care as needed

It's important to note that these services were initially poorly utilized.

Processing

- Emergency rooms provide high cost care; preventive care and continuum of care are lacking
- Physicians—Sporadic care is provided if parents don't use EPSDT
- DHS Caseworkers—Lack time to do medical case management
- Medicaid Funding—Only 10% of families secure EPSDT screening services, and subsequent services for special needs are not provided
- Parents—Do not secure preventive services or medical homes for children

OUTPUTS

Desired Outcomes

Regular, periodic preventive services and medical homes are available for all children beginning at birth.

Actual Outcomes

Only 10% of families participate in EPSDT programs and, therefore, lack preventive services and a medical home; care is secured through emergency rooms.

Output Monitors

- The federal regional office is aware of low utilization and notifies the Oklahoma Health Care Authority of needed improvements
- Oklahoma Health Care Authority stresses the need for Oklahoma State DHS to improve EPSDT utilization
- Oklahoma State DHS stresses to local county offices the need to improve EPSDT utilization

Insufficient progress is being made to accomplish desired outcomes.

Developing Alternative Solutions and Establishing Objectives

The Health Committee was heartened that there was a resource that could enable the community to make significant progress toward improving health care for low-income families. The EPSDT program would allow families to secure a medical home for their children through regular visits to a primary care physician for screenings and specialty care for specific needs identified through screenings. Further, several local private physicians agreed to work with families to implement the program and occasionally help fill gaps by providing services without charge. The Garfield County Health Department was also supportive of this initiative. The Health Committee then began to develop specific alternatives for achieving its objectives. One approach for increasing the use of EPSDT was for the DHS caseworker to:

- Give increased attention to ensure that families retain their eligibility for Medicaid
- Monitor dates for periodic screenings and encourage families to schedule appointments
- Assist families in dealing with barriers (such as transportation)

The DHS supervisor informed the Committee that DHS workers told families about the availability of EPSDT services, but caseloads prevented them from providing additional case management services. The Committee then explored ways to complement DHS services by providing case management services to inform and encourage families to use EPSDT services. The DHS supervisor initially opposed this idea based on confidentiality issues. Several Committee members knew that many low-income families attended regular WIC (supplemental nutrition program for women, infants, and children) clinics for assistance with nutrition needs. At the clinic, they often spent considerable time in waiting rooms. The Committee wondered if an outstationed case manager (from another Agency) could offer information and support on health needs. CDSA had a part-time health specialist who could:

- Help families understand the potential value of EPSDT services
- Encourage and assist them in maintaining Medicaid eligibility
- Encourage timely visits to physicians for screening and recommend follow-up services
- Deal with barriers (such as lack of transportation) to screening and follow-up services

USING A PROBLEM-SOLVING PROCESS TO GUIDE TECHNICAL AND POLITICAL ACTION

Initial Objective

The DHS supervisor initially told the Health Committee that confidentiality issues and workloads would prevent this collaborative project. Leaders of the Health Committee then approached the County DHS Director and discussed the health consequences of failure to improve EPSDT utilization and the great possibilities for broad community collaboration to address the needs. Finally, with continuing negotiation, DHS agreed to partner with CDSA on a Pilot Project named the Healthy Kids Project. The Project proposal outlined (in detail) collaborative relationships among CDSA, DHS, Garfield County Health Department, private physicians, and other providers in implementing the project.

The CDSA Health Advocate was assigned to begin work in the WIC Program waiting room to meet mothers and offer information on the potential value of EPSDT. The Advocate would also discuss resources available to them to help with barriers, including lapse of Medicaid eligibility and transportation, making and keeping periodic appointments, and other issues. The CDSA Health Advocate was very successful in increasing the usage of EPSDT. Additionally, DHS caseworkers enjoyed working with the CDSA Health Advocate and appreciated the help their caseload families were receiving. The DHS County Director and the DHS EPSDT supervisor became very supportive of the Pilot Project and a possible expansion of Healthy Kids services.

The Health Committee's initial objective for the above project was to:
- Demonstrate the value of case management services
- Significantly enhance family utilization of EPSDT and follow-up health care services
- Lay the groundwork for a grant or other funding of full-time staff to achieve as close to 100 percent utilization as possible

The duration of the pilot project was six to twelve months.

Subsequent Objective

Having succeeded at its initial objective, the CDSA Health Committee established a subsequent objective of securing funding for a full-time Healthy Steps staff person through a broadened pilot project with the Oklahoma Health Care Authority (a state agency charged with EPSDT management). Initially, the funding would be for one year, and with success, multi-year funding would follow. The Health Care Authority was very concerned about poor EPSDT in the state and was excited to learn about a locality that significantly increased utilization. The Authority approved funding for expanding the Healthy Steps initiative, which increased EPSDT utilization in the County from 10% to 80%. The DHS supervisor, who initially opposed the collaboration, advocated for the partnership and presented at a regional DHS meeting to encourage the expansion of these collaborative efforts to improve child health.

The following diagram illustrates the Enid child health care system after the CDSA initiative.

Phase 2: Child Health Care System *Following* CDSA Initiative:
Changes Leading to Benefits for Children and Families

INPUTS

DEMANDS
- Parents
- Oklahoma Health Care Authority
- DHS State Office
- Medicaid Regional Office Demands

SUPPORT
Medical Funding
- EPSDT Screenings
- Payment for Specialized Medical Needs
- OK Health Care Authority
- Funding for Healthy Kids Project
- Regional Medicaid Office
- Technical Assistance
County Director and EPSDT Supervisor
Support Collaboration COSA
- Provides Case Management
- Board Leadership
- Funds Part-Time Health Outreach Worker

SYSTEM PROCESSING

SUB-SYSTEMS
- Hospital Emergency Rooms
- Private Physicians
- Parents
- DHS Caseworkers
- Medicaid
- Healthy Kid Collaborative
  - COSA
  - DHS
  - OU Family Practice Clinic
  - Participating Private Physicians
  - Health Department

FEEDBACK

SYSTEM ENVIRONMENT

OUTPUTS

DESIRED OUTCOMES
- All eligible families receive EPSDT services, follow-up health care.

ACTUAL OUTCOMES
- 80% of eligible families receive services and have medical homes (as contrasted to 10% before Initiative)

OUTPUT MONITORS
- Medicaid Regional Office
- Oklahoma Health Care Authority
- State DHS
- CDSH Health Committee
- Family Feedback

■ indicates system changes following CDSA Initiative

SUMMARY OF SYSTEM CHANGES FROM PHASE I TO PHASE II

INPUTS

Support

- Healthy Kids Project was established to improve Child Health
- Oklahoma Health Care Authority provides funding for the Healthy Kids Project, which facilitates collaboration among Healthy Steps partners and case management services to families
- The Regional Medicaid Office supports the project and provides technical assistance
- The county DHS Director and EPSDT Supervisor strongly support collaboration and encourage other communities to adopt the model
- CDSA expands role in improving child health care systems

PROCESSING

Parents are encouraged, assisted, and reminded to ensure children secure periodic screening and follow-up care

Private Physicians

- Additional physicians offer Medicaid services
- Serve a high percentage of eligible families

Hospital Emergency Rooms

Report decreased numbers of non-emergency services to families

OUTPUTS

- The percentage of eligible families receiving services increases from 10% to 80%
- Regular family visits to primary care physicians make it possible for families to establish a medical home

CHAPTER VI

Developing and Using Political Resources

An important factor in reducing local leaders' willingness to tackle local problems is their previous negative experiences in trying to achieve change. Local leaders concerned about community health, education, and economic security often experience long-standing frustration, a sense of powerlessness, and, in some instances, apathy due to their efforts to address seemingly intractable problems. Frequently, they may have approached organizations with the authority to take needed action and gotten responses like "no problems exist" or agreement that "a need exists, but our organization lacks resources to meet it." Previous efforts to bring about change may also have seemed hopeful initially and then failed to materialize.

On the other hand, successful past experiences of leaders seeking change help to support or facilitate change within the community. The key informant survey is intended to capture these past experiences and lay the groundwork for developing strategies that make positive use of them. A major requirement for success in local empowerment is helping leaders learn both to identify their existing and potential political resources and how to deploy them to impact local decision-making.

In this chapter, we will:

- Discuss important concepts of influence and power which can help lay the groundwork for change
- Delineate alternative political resources that can increase an organization's capacity to influence local decision-making
- Discuss how the systems model can be utilized to analyze local decision-making systems and help identify effective strategies for influencing local and state decision-making
- Identify roles that the organization and its leaders can take in this process
- Provide a detailed case example that illustrates how a community utilized this approach to change local decisions

Help local leaders learn how to identify political resources and use them to impact local decision-making.

Benveniste differentiates between technical and political roles carried out by actors in the policy-making process. Technical roles include expert, specialist, analyst, and educational professional. Political roles include the persuader, coalition developer, and information interpreter (Benveniste 1972, 7–21).

A PLURALISTIC VIEW OF POWER AND INFLUENCE

Robert Dahl presents a pluralistic view of power and influence, which we will use as a foundation for our discussion (Dahl 1974). Such a view does not assume the existence of a powerful ruling elite but rather that power is situational—that different groups of individuals will be involved in bringing about a variety of decisions depending on the interests at stake. By identifying individuals engaged regularly in decision-making related to a specific issue area, one can gain insight into the power structure in that area.

Dahl postulates that individual A has power over individual B to the extent that A can get B to do something B would otherwise not do. Dahl suggested a fourfold conception of the power relationship between A and B:

1. The base or source of one actor's power over another

2. The means of instruments used in the exertion of power

3. The amount or extent of power

4. The scope or range of power

He defined an actor's base as "all the resources...that he can exploit to affect the behavior of another." Dahl states that the "amount of an actor's power can be represented by a probability statement relating to the likelihood that a given actor can influence a decision in a given issue area." The scope of power can be measured by studying the number and significance of issue areas in which the actors effectively influence. Thus, identifying an organization's political and potential resources and assessing their capacity to influence decision-making becomes an important subject of inquiry in this area. Further, Dahl points out that a base of power itself is "inert, passive." He states, "It [the base] must be exploited in some fashion if the behavior of others is to be altered." Thus, activation and means for deploying political resources are other vital areas for inquiry.

Numerous authors have attempted to identify and define the kinds of resources available to political actors. Lengthy lists—frequently overlapping—of the resources available appear in multiple publications.

This list below draws primarily from three sources: Roald F. Campbell and Tim L. Mazzoni, Michael Aiken and Paul Mott, and Guy Benveniste.

LEGAL AUTHORITY

Aiken and Mott define authority as "consent legitimately given to groups or individuals to direct certain activities and to utilize certain resources to achieve collective purposes." Legal authority refers to that authority granted through governmental processes (Aiken and Mott 1970, 3–15). Campbell points out that "authority stemming from office is bolstered by tradition; conversely, when tradition does not sustain officiality, the latter's authority may be quite weak." Persons vested with such authority have the right to decide on specific issues and, therefore, are automatically a part of the policy-making process (Campbell and Mazzoni 1972, 49).

INFORMATION CAPABILITY

Information can be utilized to justify an actor's course of action or to discredit that of an opponent. It can also be used as a source of sanctioning for influence in a specific realm of decision-making. As a political commodity, information can be exchanged for other political commodities.

SOCIAL STATUS

Campbell and Mazzoni note that "knowledgeable onlookers have long emphasized a correlation between the perceived legitimacy of political demands and the social status of their proponents." These authors quote John Walke in stating that "reasons connected with a group's claim to be represented or with its general political power appear. . . to be more significant than reasons associated with the group's lobbying activities in the legislative arena itself" (Campbell and Mazzoni 1972, 51).

ELECTORAL CAPABILITY

While the capability to convert an electoral resource base into voters is a critical variable, studies on lobbying indicate that legislators believe electoral strength is a significant factor relating to the effectiveness of interest groups.

REPUTATION FOR POWER

Actors' perception of their relative power may affect the amount of influence they exert in specific situations. If an actor is perceived to have more than he does, less effort may be made to interfere with the exercise of that power than would be made if the real dimensions of the power balance were known. Conversely, an actor may have power and fail to exert it because they do not perceive this fact.

GROUP COHESION

The degree of perceived agreement among group members affects their capability to benefit from available political resources. Benveniste discusses this under the category of "professional consensus" (Benveniste 1972, 126).

ACCESS TO THE POWERFUL

Direct contact with persons holding power allows an actor to persuade influential persons and make them allies. In addition, access to powerful individuals may give an actor indirect control over other actors, which also must relate to the powerful figures (Benveniste 1972, 120–125).

CAPABILITY FOR FORMING COALITIONS

Contact with beneficiaries, implementers, or other professionals may allow an actor to develop coalitions that are useful in influencing decision-makers. Skill in coalition formation may be an added asset.

DEPLOYING POLITICAL RESOURCES

As organizations seek to influence decision-making, they must identify and develop political resources and deploy them efficiently and effectively. This section will discuss conceptual tools to assist in this task. Two major areas will be covered:

1. Selecting Resources and Strategies
2. Selection of Organizational Roles

SELECTING RESOURCES AND STRATEGIES

The nature of the goals sought, the characteristics of the action system, and the characteristics of the target system have been discussed as significant variables to consider in selecting political resources and strategies. Garth Jones suggests a classification of techniques that are used in this study. The strategies, their definitions, and associated tactics are discussed below (Jones 1969, 115–118).

Coercive Strategies

This category of strategy and tactics is characterized by non-mutual goal setting (a goal set up by only one side), an imbalanced power relationship, and one-sided deliberativeness. These strategies rest on the application (or the threat) of physical sanctions and/or generating frustration (either through restriction of movement or controlling through force) related to satisfying human needs, such as food, sex, and comfort. Four kinds of tactics are associated with this strategy:

1. Hierarchy
2. Elite involvement
3. Pressure
4. Stress induction

Normative Strategies

This strategy emphasizes normative power as the primary source of control. Compliance rests mainly upon the internalization of values accepted as proper and legitimate. Twelve types of normative tactics are identified:

1. Participation
2. Involvement-commitment
3. Feedback
4. Displacement of values
5. External relations
6. Social awareness
7. Education/training
8. Voluntary association
9. Exposition and propagation
10. Legitimation
11. Role definition
12. Emulation

Utilitarian Strategies

Utilization strategy and tactics are characterized by control over material resources and rewards through the allocation of increased contributions, benefits, and services. These are available to the client system when it performs as prescribed by the controllers of change.

The roles below have been identified through previous empirical studies of policy-making conducted by Campbell and Mazzoni, Robert Presthus, and Benveniste. The specific role classifications and definitions for each role are also provided.

SELECTION OF ORGANIZATIONAL ROLES

Campbell and Mazzoni identify roles that actors carry out in the various functional stages of the policy-making process (Campbell and Mazzoni 1972, 13–47). These are:

1. Interest Representatives

These are actors (individuals or groups) who have interests in specific policies. When these interests are expressed to authorities, they become political demands within the system.

2. Alternative Formulators

These actors "mediate between the great range of articulated interests and the final making of authoritative decisions." They aggregate the interests of many individuals and groups and translate them into specific policy alternatives that legislators or other officials can act upon. Alternative formulators may include political parties, educational bureaucracies, and coalitions of interest groups or other actors.

3. Authoritative Decision-Makers

Some persons have the "legal right to make specific kinds of decisions." Though they may be strongly influenced or controlled by others, these actors must make legitimate policy decisions and thus have a significant role in the policy-making process.

Research conducted by Robert Presthus in community decision-making suggests that initiator and implementer roles are carried out in policy-making (Presthus 1964, 434–476).

Initiators are actors who lend their prestige or resources to a significant project in the "take off" phase. This support is generally considered essential in determining whether or not a specific project should be undertaken. Support from initiators is a crucial factor in securing agreement from other actors.

Implementers are activists or laymen who develop the broad support and involvement necessary for the project implementation.

ANALYZING AND CHANGING POLITICAL DECISION-MAKING SYSTEMS

In the last chapter, we discussed that the systems model can help analyze and address "political" and technical problems. Previously, we illustrated using the systems model for analyzing service delivery systems and developing, selecting, and implementing program and policy improvements. This chapter focuses on using the model to analyze decision-making systems and developing strategies for change. The model can be invaluable for assessing and changing decision-making structures and processes and identifying deficiencies that lead to failed policies and programs. First, the model provides a framework for looking at all prominent actors and the interaction of these actors, which leads to poor decisions. Secondly, the model can help determine what new actors, political resources, roles, and exchanges could lead to productive outcomes.

The following is a detailed case study of a community initiative that illustrates:

- Use of the systems model to help analyze the existing decision-making system and its shortfalls in responding to community needs

- Developing strategies for changing the decision-making system to achieve improved outcomes

- The organization's and its leaders' roles in achieving and securing the change.

CASE STUDY #6
The Systems Model and Community Decision-Making Systems

The following example illustrates how the systems model can help analyze existing community decision-making systems. It will also show how a local community identified and developed political resources and carried out strategies and roles to improve outcomes.

In the early stages of Community Development Support Association's (CDSA) development, the organization conducted a key informant survey of community needs. A high-priority need identified in the survey was to establish public transportation. One of CDSA's Board members was also a volunteer leader in the YWCA. The YWCA had documented the need for transportation services through a community survey but was frustrated by the lack of interest from the Enid City Council. Enid's YWCA has long advocated for public transportation for low-income families and individuals, seniors, and persons transitioning to economic self-sufficiency.

At the time, Enid had a population of 50,000 but no public transportation system. After reviewing the City's decision-making system on public transportation and the City's failure to respond to requests for action, CDSA established a Transportation Committee to study the situation and make recommendations to the Board for action. The Committee included a local attorney active in various civic organizations, a faculty member of the Phillips University Seminary, a neighborhood association member, and an owner of a local business. The Committee's first step was to meet with the City's Assistant City Manager, who expressed that the Council had little interest in developing public transportation because "everyone in Enid has a car" and "a bus system could not generate sufficient ridership to be economically feasible."

Having seen the YWCA survey results documenting the need, the Transportation Committee was not deterred and asked to make a presentation to the Enid City Council. The City Manager agreed, and the Transportation Committee made the case for public transportation at the city council meeting. A few of the council members responded with some of the sentiments that the Committee had heard from the Assistant City Manager. At times, this meeting became heated when the Phillips University Seminary member on CDSA's Committee challenged a resistant Council member's facts.

The CDSA Transportation Committee then reviewed the City's response and began developing a plan for further action to change decision-making by the Council. The Phase I Chart uses a systems diagram to illustrate the City's decision-making system around transportation at the beginning of CDSA's initiative.

ILLUSTRATION OF CHANGING DECISION–MAKING SYSTEMS: PUBLIC TRANSPORTATION, CITY OF ENID

The following diagrams illustrate the *three phases* of the City of Enid's decision-making system on public transportation, beginning before CDSA's initiative and ending with a sustained transportation system in place.

Phase 1: Public Transportation Decision-Making System Before CDSA Initiative

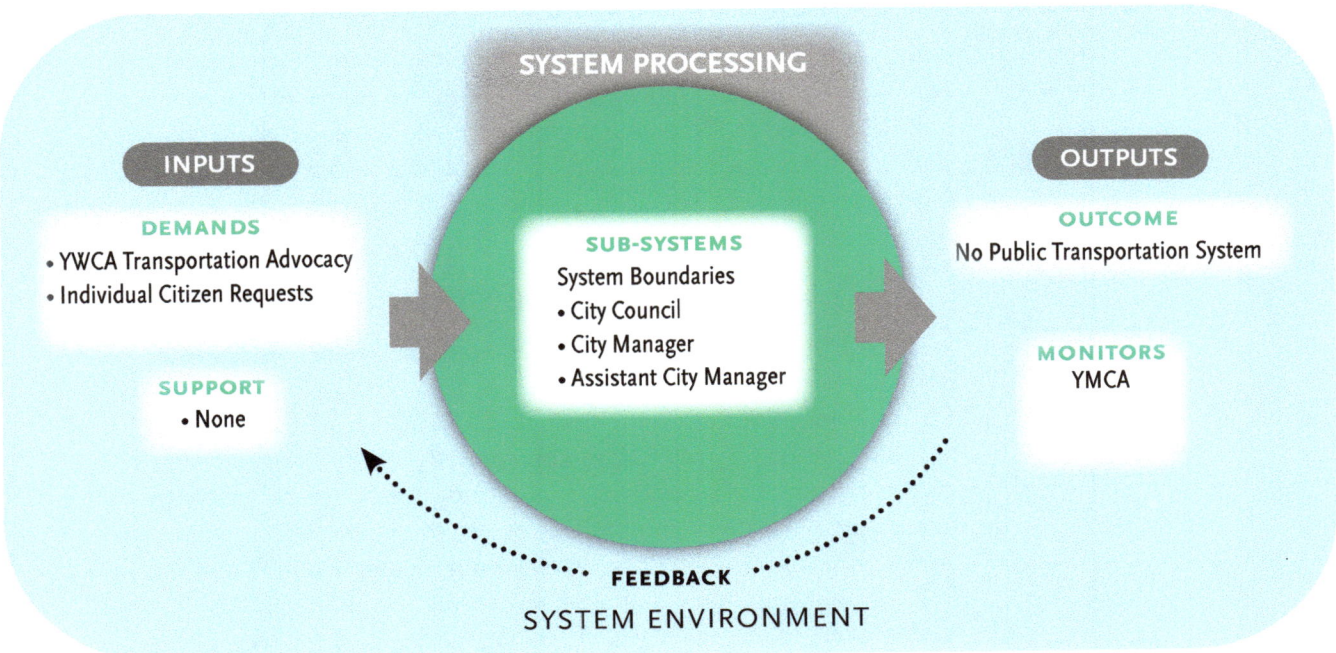

DISCUSSION OF PHASE I CHART

Before the CDSA initiative, input (demands) included the YWCA's persistent requests for the City of Enid to take action. There were also occasional requests from individual citizens. No inputs (supports—such as funding) existed since no program existed. Decision processing included the City Council, City Manager, and Assistant City Manager. The system output was that no public transportation system was in place, and there were no plans for one. The only feedback monitor was the YWCA community advocacy on transportation needs. Feedback was limited to the YWCA's contacts with city officials.

CASE STUDY #6 CONTINUES
CDSA ACTION TO CHANGE DECISION-MAKING

Transportation Committee Identifies Political Resources

Reviewing the organization's political resources, the Committee knew that CDSA lacked legal authority to put public transportation in place. CDSA, at this point, lacked electoral capability (in the case of replacing Council members who failed to act.) CDSA's short life as an organization did not offer a reputation of power. At the same time, the organization did have information capability (the YWCA survey and CDSA survey.) CDSA could form coalitions, as the organization had assembled a broad, articulate coalition of concerned local leaders. Group cohesion was an asset as both CDSA and the Transportation Committee were unified in support of public transportation. Some additional political resources could come from individual members' social status and access to people with influence and political resources/connections.

Selecting and Implementing a Strategy

In reviewing its political resources, the Committee chose primarily a normative strategy, detailed below.

The Transportation Committee, which was unsuccessful in its initial approach to the City of Enid, re-approached the City Manager with a proposal that the city establish its own Transportation Committee to study needs and alternatives and propose action to the Council. Members of the City's Transportation Committee would include Council members, CDSA's Transportation Committee representatives, and citizens interested in transportation needs. The City Manager presented the proposal to the Council, and the Council adopted it. The Council allocated funds to employ a transportation consultant to study needs and potential demand and work with the Committee to make recommendations to the Council. (At this point, there was no assumption the Committee would recommend establishing a public transportation program.)

The CDSA viewed this action as a positive step in addressing the problem. To accomplish this progress, CDSA used a normative strategy that included the following tactics:

- Participation (developing a cohesive, broad-based community coalition)

- Involvement/Commitment (seeking formulation of a City Transportation Committee)

- Legitimation (City employment of a transportation consultant and use of YWCA research)

- CDSA's potential use of political resources of access to the powerful and electoral capability (though its linkages with important constituent groups may also have helped support the initiative)

City Study and Action on Transportation
Needs and Alternatives

The transportation consultant employed by the City of Enid conducted a detailed study of transportation needs, alternatives, and funding sources. The study confirmed both the need and potential demand for transportation services. The consultant recommended that the city establish a City Transportation Authority to administer the program. The consultant also recommended a "demand responsive" shared ride taxi model for delivery of transportation services (using vans) rather than a "fixed route" bus system. The study showed that this model would be more appropriate for local needs when considering financial feasibility and customer service than a "fixed route" system. Financing sources would include state transportation funding, fees, and possible contract revenue. The consultant discussed study recommendations in detail with the newly formed City Transportation Committee, which approved the recommendations. City officials acted to establish the Enid Public Transportation Authority and began service.

Local residents received the city's new transportation program with great appreciation, which was expressed through the broad use of the service. The Enid Transportation Authority membership initially included membership from the CDSA Transportation Committee. The positive relationships between CDSA and the city grew over the years, including collaborations to expand affordable housing and address other local needs.

CDSA Organizational Roles in Change

The CDSA Transportation Committee performed both:

- The role of interest representative for multiple constituent groups seeking to fill the need for public transportation

- The role of alternative formulator in developing a productive way for the City of Enid and CDSA, along with other interest groups, to end the standoff about public transportation in Enid. (The alternative presented was for the city to appoint city transportation officials to do an in-depth exploration of needs and potential demand for services, alternative delivery systems, financial feasibility and sources of financing, and management of the system.)

The Committee also performed the following:

- Initiator role in reopening the demands for public transportation
- Implementer roles with members serving both on the City Transportation Committee and the new City Transportation Authority
- Political roles that included persuader and coalition developer

Phase 2: Initial Changes in Public Transportation Decision-Making System and Impact on Outcomes

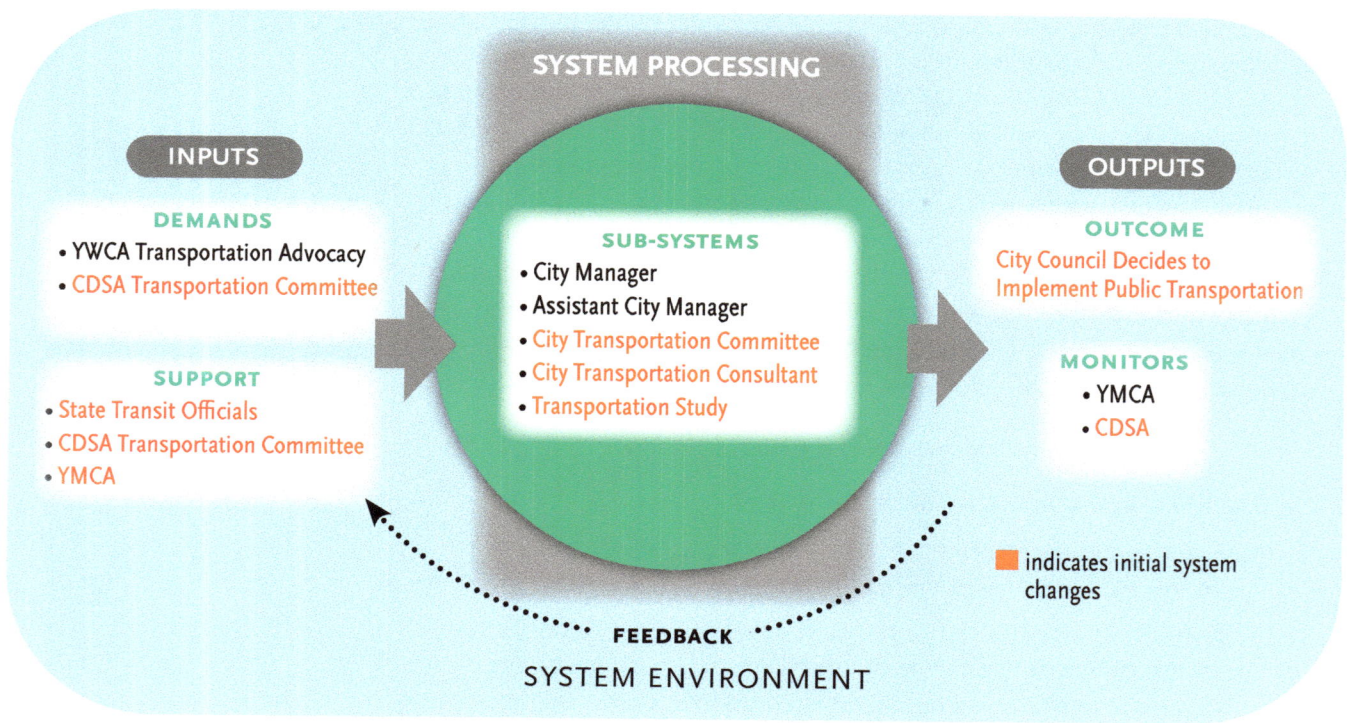

DISCUSSION OF PHASE II CHART

This diagram illustrates how initiatives by CDSA and subsequent actions by City officials led to changes in the City's decision-making system and the resulting decision to establish a City Transportation System.

A change in inputs (CDSA Transportation Committee) whose members were:

- Leaders of key constituencies who were armed with information from the YWCA study
- Committed to securing public transportation
- Provided with access to City officials

Processing of demands changed when:

- There was an intensive debate between CDSA members and resistant Council members, and there was persistent contact and alternatives presented by CDSA Committee members
- The City Manager and Council agreed to develop a City Transportation Committee, have a transportation consultant, and conduct a study (the Committee included Council members, CDSA, and other community leaders)
- The City Transportation Committee and transportation consultant were added to decision-making sub-systems

CASE STUDY #6 CONTINUES

Further, the City's study of needs and feasibility led to the consultant recommending an innovative approach related to Enid's specific needs. Rather than traditional bus routes, which appeared to have feasibility draw-backs, the consultant recommended a "shared ride" type of system. New input to the study from Oklahoma Department of Public Transportation officials confirmed that this was a viable approach and that state funding would be available for a portion of the costs. The city's decision to establish a transportation system also created supportive input from various community leaders (including the YWCA and CDSA) who had previously expressed considerable frustration.

System Output changed from the city's refusal to act on public transportation to its agreement to establish a Transportation System.

Changes in Output Monitors include Enid Transportation Authority data on local utilization of services and customer needs and feedback, which becomes ongoing input for Transportation System decision-making.

The following diagram illustrates additional changes in the decision-making process following the establishment of a transportation system in Enid.

Phase 3: Public Transportation Decision-Making System at Project Conclusion and Impact on Outcomes

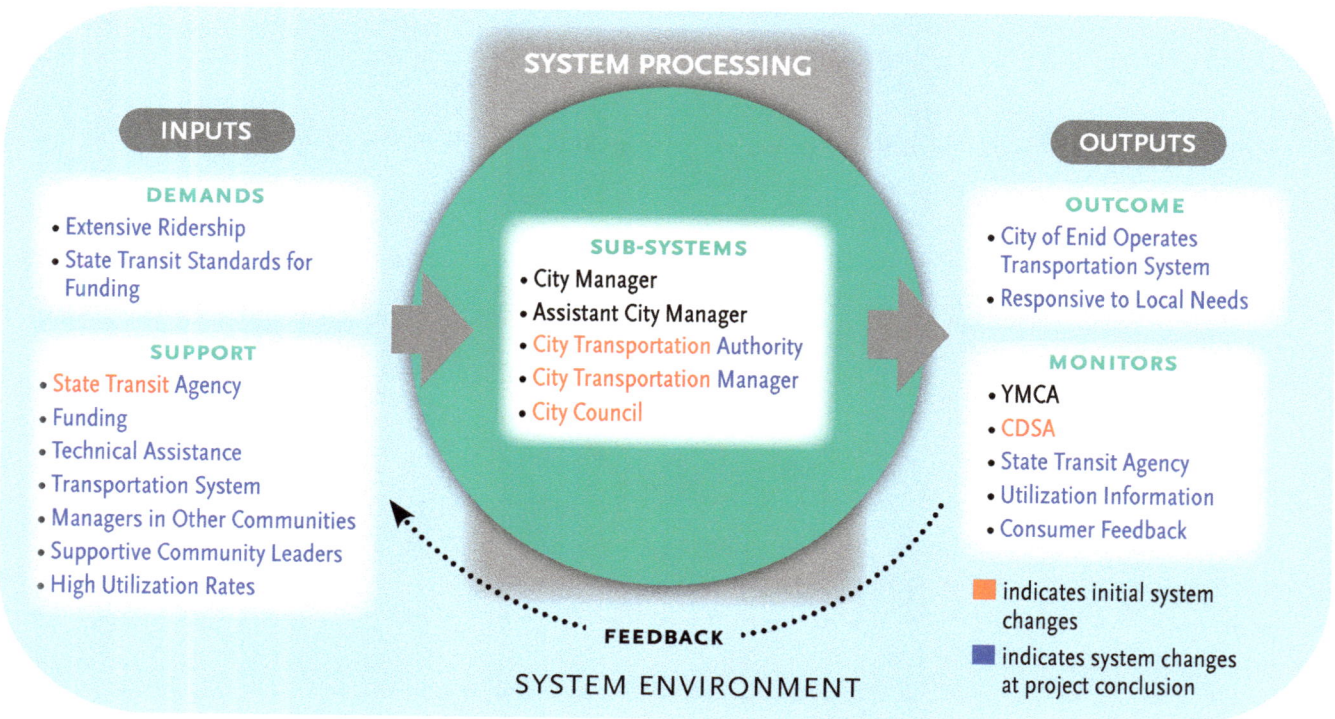

DISCUSSION OF PHASE III CHART

The illustration above shows important changes in all elements of the city's decision-making system on transportation.

Input changes included high utilization rates, which were both demands and support for the system. State standards were a demand.

Support for the system came from customers and leaders who greatly valued the services. The Oklahoma Department of Transportation provided funding and technical assistance. Further, the Enid Transportation Manager received helpful information from managers of other communities about alternative ways to address service and funding issues.

The decision-processing sub-systems were greatly enhanced by the existence of:

- A fully funded transportation program, managers, and staff
- A Transit Authority Board made up of community leaders committed to providing accessible and high-quality services
- Management staff who could continually assess utilization, unique local needs, and funding strategies to make the system responsible and sustainable

Output changes included sustained and expanded operation of a transportation system responsive to local needs.

FEEDBACK

Data on customer utilization, customer satisfaction, and additional service requests became ongoing sources of feedback for the decision-making system.

CHAPTER VII

Developing and Using Technical Capacity to Achieve and Sustain Improved Outcomes

At the heart of effective planning and action organizations is a core of people (volunteers and staff) who are fully in tune with community needs and are passionate about action to relieve suffering and provide opportunities for all community residents.

Achieving desired outcomes requires local planning and action organizations to continue focusing on developing and using both technical and political capacities. This is the responsibility of the total organization. Therefore, both the Board and staff need a set of complementary technical capabilities and roles. In a healthy organization, this technical capacity is continually evolving to meet the organization's challenges. This chapter outlines the technical capacities, needs, and a process for developing these capacities.

This chapter focuses on the characteristics of these technical capacities and the importance of Board and staff attention to the development and use of these capacities in every phase of initiatives to improve community outcomes—from the initial engagement of community leaders through policy and program implementation, evaluation, and action to sustain progress.

The importance of sustained attention to technical capacity can be illustrated in cases where communities have made substantial investments to secure approval and financing of an evidence-based program but find that desired outcomes are not being achieved. This could occur for many reasons, including:

- An insufficiently researched program was funded and not effective in producing desired results
- An evidence-based program was secured, but the organization did not implement the program with fidelity or didn't take unique local infrastructure or population characteristics into account in the implementation
- The community is unable to sustain the program long enough to demonstrate its effectiveness

Local planning and action organizations need the technical capacity to:
- Put in place policies and programs that have demonstrated effectiveness in achieving desired outcomes and take into account local population and infrastructure
- Help ensure the implementation of programs and policies with fidelity and sustainability
- Have built-in evaluations and processes for making needed adjustments in delivery

Board and staff members must be aware of these requirements as the organization begins initiatives. While all of these cannot be achieved immediately in many areas, steps to make this happen must begin on "Day 1".

The good news is that while planning to achieve these technical requirements takes considerable discipline and time, achieving positive outcomes can bring energy, excitement, and confidence to the organization's Board, staff, and membership.

TECHNICAL CORE AND TECHNICAL TEAMS

For each project or policy domain, planning and action organizations need teams of people who have the knowledge, experience, and skills to carry out the problem-solving process in a way that achieves desired outcomes.

These technical teams (which may function as committees) are needed for each major project domain and address technical and political requirements for achieving goals. They draw on their experience, knowledge, and skills in making decisions and taking action in every step of the problem-solving process—from developing a sound problem statement based on the needs of the community, to problem analysis and selection of sound interventions, to program evaluation and modification and sustained improvement in outcomes.

The organization's "technical core" will include Board members, membership body members, partners, and consultants (volunteer and/or paid) as appropriate. The technical core includes persons needed to help the community plan, deliver, and sustain improved outcomes.

This chapter will focus on two significant aspects of developing this technical core:

1. The organization's capacity to recruit and support Board and staff persons who can perform important technical roles to improve community outcomes. Attention will be given to specific values and skills, knowledge, and experience needed to achieve these roles.

2. The organization's capacity to assist the community in identifying and sustaining programs and policies which are effective in achieving desired outcomes.

PROFESSIONAL STAFF AS A SOURCE OF TECHNICAL CAPACITY

This section will deal with the professional staff component of the organization's technical core. Three key participants in the initial technical core are discussed below.

Lead Organizer

Essentially, the lead organizer's overall role is to engage support from community leaders in accomplishing the processes outlined in the Model for Community Empowerment outlined in Chapter III. In practical terms, the organizer helps the local community take increasingly influential roles in ensuring the health and economic well-being of all community residents.

As noted throughout the book, much of the political and technical capacity will come from the community and external sources it can access. Empowerment is rooted in democracy, and inclusive participation in planning and action is fundamental to mobilizing these capacities.

The following is a summary of key roles and capacities the lead organizer can bring and education and information sources that can contribute to these capacities.

1. *Listener, Citizen Engager, and Organization Builder*

   Knowledge and skills for this role were discussed in detail in Chapters IV and V. Knowledge and skills include community research, capacity to support volunteers in carrying out the Model outlined in this book, and nonprofit management.

2. *Coalition Builder*

   Project by project knowledge and skills for this role were covered in Chapter VI: Developing and Using Political Resources. Knowledge sources include political science and community organization.

3. *Innovator in Policy, Programs, and Financing*

   Knowledge and skills in this role were covered in Chapter IV: Using a Problem-Solving Process. The systems model can assist with problem analysis, developing innovative alternatives, and technical and policy problems. Accessing and using information on evidence-based programs is also critical to innovation at the local level. Knowledge and skill sources include system theory, program development, scientific method, website development, and partnership building.

4. *Partnership Builder*

   In most instances, building and maintaining effective partnerships is critical to achieving the objectives and goals of planning and action for nonprofits. Numerous authors have spelled out the conditions necessary for effective partners—shared interest, complementary resources, and mechanisms for implementing partnerships.

5. *Manager of Implementation, Sustainability Planning, Evaluation Research, and Policy and Program Adjustment*

As noted many times in this publication, the primary incentive that local leaders have for participating in planning and action organizations is sustained improvement to community health and economic security for its citizens. A key role of the lead organizer is to ensure that action is taken to implement plans and that sustainability and evaluation research is built into all projects. Taking the long view on the front end can build in necessary resources to achieve progressive improvements in policies, programs, and outcomes.

Chief Financial Officer

An experienced and creative chief financial officer who supports the organization's mission is vital to the organization. Planning and action organizations are always in the business of helping communities secure, redirect, and manage financial resources to achieve improved outcomes. Further, these organizations must find dependable and ever-changing resources for internal operations. Innovative solutions frequently involve partnerships among multiple secure delivery organizations and multiple funders. Annual organizational fundraisers may also be a part of the mix. In addition, nonprofits must meet IRS standards and yearly reporting deadlines and fulfill agreements with partners and multiple funders. Staff payrolls and associated reporting, trust, and integrity in all these relationships are essential. The Chief Financial Officer can provide leadership and support in choosing objectives in all of these areas. An "in-house" chief financial officer in a senior management role and participating in day-to-day organizational decision-making can play a significant role in making the organization more responsive and effective in meeting community needs.

Investment in this staff position is a high priority. In an organization's early development, when total resources are minimal, a contract for basic accounting services may suffice, particularly if the contractor is qualified and very supportive of the organization's mission. As organizational funding sources increase and become more numerous, an "in-house" professional fiscal officer is needed.

TIPS FOR ESTABLISHING AND MAINTAINING MULTIPLE PARTNERSHIPS

Carefully listen to potential partners and ascertain whether or not there are shared interests and complementary resources

Determine if the potential partner is interested and/or views the partnership as a priority

Create detailed written agreements about how the partnership will work to achieve mutual objectives.

Develop structures and create procedures to deal with problems quickly

Ensure the partnership is supported by appropriate decision-makers in both organizations

Monitor mutual benefits by the lead organizer on an ongoing basis

Recognize and celebrate partner contributions at annual meetings, media releases, etc.

Organize regular meetings of partners to monitor progress and make modifications as needed

DEVELOPING AND USING TECHNICAL CAPACITY TO ACHIEVE AND SUSTAIN IMPROVED OUTCOMES

Board and Committee Members as Sources of Technical Capacity

As mentioned in Chapter II in the section on Organization Structure, the Board needs to include persons who bring competencies in one or more of the following areas:

1. Knowledge of local needs

2. Developing and implementing plans to meet objectives

3. Securing linkages with persons and/or organizations that can help influence community decision-making

Technical knowledge of Board member skills can complement those of professional staff and accelerate the movement toward improving outcomes. There are many examples of the value of volunteer contributions to an organization's technical capacity. Committee members and membership body members can also make technical contributions. A few examples of technical contributions of volunteer leaders are discussed below.

EXAMPLE 1
Early Childhood Development

The Community Development Support Association in Enid, Oklahoma, was instrumental in establishing the Parents As Teachers program (an early childhood program focusing on school readiness) both in northern Oklahoma and statewide. A CDSA Board member who was a pediatrician and a strong advocate for preventive programs (particularly early childhood programs) was part of the Health Com-mittee, which identified this need as a priority. A participant in CDSA's membership body, who was also a member of the Enid School Board and had been researching evidence-based early childhood programs, recommended to CDSA's Executive Director that the organization explore establishing the Parents As Teachers program in Enid.

The Executive Director and Board members were very impressed with the program, and the Board of Directors acted to establish a local program initially with private funding. The community response to the program was very positive, and the agency sought public funding alternatives. One membership body member was a State Senator who provided technical assistance and leadership in securing state funding. The long-term result was the establishment of a statewide Parents As Teachers program.

EXAMPLE 2
Health Care

A second example (discussed previously) is the Lead Nurse of the Oklahoma University Family Medicine Clinic, who provided technical information that laid the groundwork for expanding local health care for low-income families through the Early Periodic Screening and Diagnostic Testing Program. The nurse first provided information about the lack of medical homes for large numbers of families (who used hospital emergency rooms as their primary source of care). She pointed out the low usage (10%) of the EPSDT program, which helps families secure a medical home, schedule preventive screenings, and get care for problems identified through the screenings. As a result of this work, the Healthy Kids collaborative was established and increased EPSDT utilization of eligible families from 10% to 80%.

EXAMPLE 3
Juvenile Services

Finally, a respected public sector attorney who received an appointment as a juvenile judge found the system lacked adequate support services for youth and families involved with the court. The juvenile judge brought these shortfalls and the related consequences to the attention of community leaders. She took the lead in forming the Children & Family Council of Oklahoma County. Her leadership led to the establishment of the Family Tree program, which is located on the Juvenile Justice Center campus. The program was easily accessible to youth and families involved with the court, and it provided a full range of vital community services to assist youth and family needs.

In each of the above case examples, the volunteer leaders provided years of technical assistance that helped to design, fund, implement, and evaluate the community program initiatives.

CHAPTER VIII

Securing Investment in Planning and Action Nonprofits

Previous chapters provide research and numerous case examples illustrating the great need and potential for community empowerment through effective planning and action organizations. A model for organizing and implementing broad planning and action organizations has also been discussed extensively. This chapter summarizes and expands upon previous examples of avenues for securing needed resources. Two major kinds of investments include:

1. Investment of time and talent by volunteer leaders who are passionate about improving local health, education, and income security outcomes

2. Financial investment in local planning and action organizations

SECURING INVESTMENTS OF TIME AND TALENT

Chapters III and IV outline approaches for securing and sustaining engaged volunteers and provide core examples. As emphasized in these chapters, the engagement of volunteer leaders who have direct experience with deficiencies and the consequences of inadequate community opportunities, knowledge about alternative solutions, and the capacity to help influence decisions is central to success in local empowerment.

Early in the organization's development, key informant surveys can help identify and secure engaged and volunteer leaders. As the organization matures, the organization's nominating committee and Board can take the lead in expanding and strengthening volunteer involvement. Citizen involvement in program evaluation and periodic community needs surveys can help update the organizational focus on actions required to improve outcomes and help sustain and expand volunteer engagement.

SECURING FINANCIAL INVESTMENT

The following is a summary of sources for financing a local planning and action organization, which were discussed in the Introduction and subsequent chapters. While this list is not all-inclusive, it does provide some helpful ideas for initial funding.

Local Fundraisers

Successful local fundraisers can signal community support for the project to foundations, public agencies, and other potential funding sources. Fundraisers can also provide initial incomes to meet start-up costs, including part-time staff and funds that can be matched with other income sources to help meet objectives and opportunities to "get the word out" on benefits to local residents. Some organization-backed fundraisers are built around an annual event that local residents look forward to attending.

Many of the organizations discussed in the Introduction and in case examples conducted successful annual fundraisers, accomplishing most of the above mentioned objectives. Two of the previously discussed organizations—the Step-Up Program for Homeless Youth and the Lincoln County Coalition for Child Wellbeing—hosted fundraisers that exceeded their goals.

Local Foundations

Local foundations are another excellent support for financial investment in planning and action organizations. Foundations want to invest in priority needs and organizations that can deliver positive benefits to communities. The Avedis Foundation's investment in helping the local Community Action Agency deal with a significant financial and management crisis discussed in the Introduction is an excellent example of such an investment. The Foundation received a request for assistance from the agency and contacted the Caring Communities Support Center to conduct an agency study with recommendations for dealing with the financial crises and strengthening management and services in a six-county area. Caring Communities consultation was intensive and continued until the objectives were successfully implemented. Foundations can be helpful in various ways, including linkages and partnerships with other funders to achieve local goals.

Public Sources

Some publicly funded initiatives involve the engagement of Board leaders in developing local policies and programs that respond effectively to local needs. The organizations discussed in the Introduction received substantial federal and state resources to improve health, education, and income security outcomes. The Community Council of Central Oklahoma, the Community Development Support Association, and the Central Oklahoma Community Action Agency are examples of organizations that secure substantial public funding.

The United Way

Many United Way organizations have recognized the importance of volunteer-driven planning and action to deal with a wide range of community Needs. The Community Council of Central Oklahoma example in the Introduction illustrates an organization that received annual funding for its core budget from the United Way. As noted in the illustration, the Community Council of Central Oklahoma was an autonomous agency with funding from both public and private sources. In recent years, some United Ways have provided planning services directly rather than funding a separate planning agency. In some communities, funding for broad community planning and action is not offered by the United Way. Regardless of the situation, United Way can be an excellent partner, whether as a funder of a planning and action organization or as a collaborator in initiating and sustaining planning initiatives.

REFERENCES

1. Atkins, Robert, Sarah Allred, and Daniel Hart. "Philanthropy's Rural Blind Spot." *Stanford Social Innovation Review* 19, no. 2 (2021): 26-33. https://doi.org/10.48558/FC9E-0X43.

2. Freeman, Jo. "The Tyranny of Structurelessness." *Berkeley Journal of Sociology* 17, (1972): 151-164.

3. "Key Informant Approach." Program Development and Evaluation-Division of Extension. University of Wisconsin-Madison, 2017. Weblink: https://fyi.extension.wisc.edu/programdevelopment/files/2017/07/keyinform.pdf.

4. Faifua, Denise. *The Key Informant Technique in Qualitative Research.* Sage Research Methods Cases Part 1, SAGE Publications, Ltd., 2014. https://doi.org/10.4135/978144627305014540254.

5. Dahl, Robert A. *Who Governs? Democracy and Power in an American City.* 1st ed. New Haven and London: Yale University Press, 1974.

6. Aiken, Michael, and Paul E. Mott. T*he Structure of Community Power.* New York: Random House, 1970.

7. Campbell, Roald F. and Tim L. Mazzoni Jr. *"The Governance of Education: A Progress Report."* Paper presented at "Big Six" annual meeting, Chicago, Illinois, December 4, 1972. Weblink: https://files.eric.ed.gov/fulltext/ED073521.pdf.

8. Benveniste, Guy. *The Politics of Expertise.* Berkeley: Glendessary Press, 1972.

9. Jones, Garth. *Planned Organizational Change: A Study in Change Dynamics.* New York: Praeger, 1969.

10. Presthus, Robert. *Men at the Top: A Study in Community Power.* New York: Oxford University Press, 1964.

APPENDIX
BYLAWS EXAMPLE

[ORGANIZATION NAME]
BYLAWS
ARTICLE I
NAME AND IDENTIFICATION

Section I. Name

The name of this organization shall be [ORGANIZATION NAME], ([ORGANIZATION ACRONYM]).

Section II. Status

[ORGANIZATION NAME], is a voluntary, nonprofit corporation chartered with the State of Oklahoma and qualified as a charitable, tax-exempt organization under section 501(c)(3) of the Internal Revenue Code. [ORGANIZATION NAME]'s fiscal year begins July 1 and ends June 30.

ARTICLE II
MISSION AND PURPOSE

Section I. Mission Statement

A. [ORGANIZATION NAME]'s mission is to improve health, education, and economic outcomes for Oklahoma families. It will accomplish this by supporting local leaders in Oklahoma communities in improving local outcomes by building local infrastructure, and through collaboration with leaders in other communities to influence policies and programs within the State of Oklahoma in ways that make them more responsive and effective.

Section II. Purpose

A. The corporation's purposes shall be as stated in its articles of incorporation.

ARTICLE III
TIME AND PLACE OF MEETINGS

[ORGANIZATION NAME], as an organization receiving public funds, follows the Oklahoma Open Meeting Act.

Section I. Annual Meeting

There shall be an annual meeting of the [ORGANIZATION NAME], to be held each June, subject to postponement by the board. If the annual meeting is postponed, a special meeting may be held in its place, and any business transacted shall have the same force and effect as if transacted at the annual meeting.

The purposes of the annual meeting are:

    A. To provide information to the public regarding [ORGANIZATION ACRONYM]'s purpose and accomplishments in the previous year;

    B. To receive the annual report of the Board of Directors;

    C. To install new members of the Board of Directors, and to elect officers for the coming year;

    D. To recognize the efforts of [ORGANIZATION ACRONYM] staff and other community members.

Section II. Regular Meetings

Regular meetings of the board shall be held at least six (6) times per year on such dates and at such times and places as the board may determine.

Section III. Special Meetings

Special meetings of the board may be called by the Board Chair as required and as allowed by Oklahoma Open Meeting Laws.

ARTICLE IV
BOARD OF DIRECTORS

Section I. Governing Authority

The corporation's Board of Directors shall supervise, control, and direct the finances, business, and affairs of the corporation. All members of the board shall fully participate in the development, planning, implementation, and evaluation of the programs offered by the corporation.

Section II. Composition and Selection

The Board of Directors shall be composed of up to fifteen (15) members with voting authority and up to five (5) ex-officio members without voting authority. Board members shall include community leaders of Oklahoma communities with an interest in and capacity for helping achieve the organization's mission. The Nominating Committee will nominate persons to serve on the Board of Directors at the annual meeting and to fill vacancies which occur between annual meetings.

Members of the board may not vote by proxy.

Section III. Terms of Service

    A. The term of service shall be three (3) years.

        a. Consecutive terms – Board members who are elected/ selected for three-year terms can serve no more than two (2) consecutive terms and may not be re-seated on the board until a minimum of one (1) year has elapsed following completion of their two (2) consecutive terms.

b. Commencement of term – Term of membership begins with the installation of new members at the annual meeting.

c. Ad Interim members – Members filling unexpired terms are subject to the term to which they are elected/selected and may only complete one additional term after completion of the unexpired term.

B. Grounds for Removal of Directors

a. Incapacity – The board may remove a director if, in the opinion of the board, the director is incapacitated or otherwise unable to carry out the duties of their office.

b. Cause – The Board of Directors may remove a director for cause for one or more of the following reasons: conduct the board deems contrary to the best interests of the corporation; violations of the corporation's articles of incorporation, bylaws, conflict of interest policy, board resolutions, or other policies; absence from three (3) or more consecutive board meetings; repeated disruptions of board and/or committee meetings; or false statements on documents completed in connection with service as a director of the corporation.

c. Removal Procedures – The board shall provide all directors, including the director proposed to be removed, with at least 48 hours' notice of the meeting at which the removal is to be considered. The notice must specify that a purpose of the meeting is to consider removal of the director. The director proposed to be removed shall be entitled to an opportunity to be heard at the meeting. A majority vote of a quorum of the board is required for removal.

d. Resignation of Directors – A director may resign by delivering their written letter of resignation to the President of the board, to a meeting of the directors, or to the corporation at its principal office. The resignation shall be effective upon receipt unless specified to be effective at some other time. A director who has ceased to meet the qualifications for service as a director, as specified in these bylaws and by the board from time to time, and/or for the board seat to which the individual was elected is deemed to have resigned as of the date they ceased to meet those qualifications.

Section IV. Quorum and Parliamentary Procedure

A. Quorum – The required quorum shall be more than fifty percent of the current total voting membership on the board for transaction of business at any meeting.

B. Parliamentary Procedures – Robert's Rules of Order shall be utilized in the conduct of Caring Communities Support Center's meetings.

Section V. Code of Conduct/Duality of Interest

The Code of Conduct for officers, employees, and agents of [ORGANIZATION ACRONYM] is described in detail in agency policies and includes prohibitions of:

A. Nepotism

B. Conflict of Interest and Duality of Interest

C. Discriminatory Practices

Section VI. Compensation of Directors

A. Directors may not receive compensation for serving on the corporation's Board of Directors or for providing services to the corporation. However, they may receive reimbursement or advances from the corporation for reasonable and documented expenses incurred in the course of performing services as directors or officers. To the extent the corporation makes any such reimbursements or advances, it shall do so only in accordance with financial policies established from time to time by the board.

Section VII. Executive Director

A. The Board of Directors shall appoint and employ an Executive Director who, subject to the board's direction and control, shall: manage the day-to-day affairs of the corporation; implement goals and policies established by the board; and report on and advise the board and its committees concerning the affairs and activities of the corporation. The Executive Director shall be empowered to hire, supervise, and terminate the corporation's other employees in accordance with personnel policies established by the board. In addition, the Executive Director shall perform such other duties and have such other powers as the board may determine from time to time. The board shall evaluate the Executive Director and set their compensation on an annual basis. The Executive Director may attend meetings of the board and its committees unless excluded by a majority vote of the board or committee at a meeting at which a quorum is present or by a policy established by the board. The board may remove the Executive Director at any time with or without cause. Removal without cause shall be without prejudice to the Executive Director's contract rights, if any, and the appointment of the Executive Director shall not itself create contract rights.

ARTICLE V
OFFICERS

Section I. Officers

A. The Officers of the [ORGANIZATION NAME], shall be a President, Vice President, and Secretary/Treasurer, each of whom shall be members of the Board of Directors and each of whom shall be elected by the board. No director shall hold more than one office at the same time.

B. The Nominating Committee will develop recommendations for officers and present these to the board. Officers shall take office immediately following election and serve until the close of the term or until successors are elected.

Section II. Terms of Office

A. The officers shall be elected for a term of one (1) year.

Section III. Ad Interim Vacancies

A. Ad interim vacancies of the [ORGANIZATION NAME], officers shall be filled by the Board of Directors, and the person or persons elected shall hold office for the remainder of the unexpired term.

Section IV. Duties of Officers

A. President – The President shall: (1) be the chief volunteer officer of the corporation, subject to the direction and control of the board; (2) preside at meetings of the Board of Directors; and (3) perform such other duties and have such other powers as the Board of Directors may determine from time to time. The President shall be ex-officio on all committees.

B. Vice President – In the absence of the President or in the event of the President's inability or refusal to act, the Vice President shall perform the duties of the President and when so acting shall have all the powers of and be subject to all the restrictions upon the President. The Vice President shall also perform such other duties and have such other powers as the Board of Directors may determine from time to time.

C. Secretary/Treasurer – The Secretary/Treasurer shall see to the recording and maintenance of records of all proceedings of the Board of Directors, including the attendance of directors at meetings in documents kept for that purpose, which shall be kept at the principal office of the corporation and which shall be open at all reasonable times for the inspection of any director. The Secretary/Treasurer shall preside over meetings of the personnel and finance committee and oversee the corporation's financial management practices through the personnel and finance committee, subject to the direction and control of the Board of Directors. The Secretary/Treasurer may perform other duties and have such other powers as the directors shall determine from time to time.

Section V. Grounds for Removal of Officers

A. Incapacity – The board may remove an officer if, in the opinion of the board, the officer is incapacitated or otherwise unable to carry out the duties of their office.

B. Cause – The Board of Directors may remove an officer for cause for one or more of the following reasons: conduct the board deems contrary to the best interests of the corporation; violations of the corporation's articles of incorporation, bylaws, conflict of interest policy, board resolutions, or other policies; absence from three (3) or more consecutive board meetings; repeated disruptions of board and/or committee meetings; or false statements on documents completed in connection with service as a member of the Board of Directors of the corporation.

C. Removal Procedures – The board shall provide all board members, including the officer proposed to be removed, with at least 48 hours' notice of the meeting at which the removal is to be considered. The notice must specify that a purpose of the meeting is to consider removal of the officer. The officer proposed to be removed shall be entitled to an opportunity to be heard at the meeting. A majority vote of a quorum of the board is required for removal.

D. Resignation of Officers – An officer may resign by delivering their written letter of resignation to the President of the board, to a meeting of the board, or to the corporation at its principal office. The resignation shall be effective upon receipt unless specified to be effective at some other time. An officer who has ceased to meet the qualifications for service as an officer, as specified in these bylaws and by the board from time to time, and/or for the board seat to which they were elected is deemed to have resigned as of the date the individual ceased to meet those qualifications.

ARTICLE VI

COMMITTEES

Section I. Committee Structure

A. The committees of [ORGANIZATION NAME], shall be of two (2) types: Ad Hoc and Standing Committees. Ad Hoc Committees shall be created by the board for a definite and specific purpose not within the purview of any standing committee, and for a stated period of time. Standing Committees shall consist of other committees that may be required for the administrative or functional work of the [ORGANIZATION NAME]

B. The President and board shall refer all [ORGANIZATION NAME], affairs and business requiring committee action to the proper committee. If it is a matter outside the duty and scope of any Standing Committee, the matter shall be referred to an Ad Hoc Committee created for that purpose.

C. All actions of both the Standing and Ad Hoc Committees must be ratified by the Board of Directors.

Section II. Standing Committees

The Chairperson of each committee must be a member of the Board of Directors. Committee members may be selected community-wide, and are eligible for reappointment. Chairpersons may serve only three (3) consecutive one-year terms.

There shall be the following standing committees:

A. Nominating Committee

a. Composition – There shall be a Nominating Committee composed of a Chairman and a minimum of three (3) additional persons.

b. Board Selection – The Nominating Committee shall nominate members for the Board of Directors

c. Officer Selection – It shall submit a slate of officers to the Board of Directors at the first board meeting following the annual meeting. Officers shall take office immediately following the election and serve until the close of the one-year term.

d. Ad Interim Vacancies – Nominees to fill ad interim vacancies of board officer positions shall be submitted to the board by the Nominating Committee, and the person or persons elected shall serve for the remainder of the unexpired term.

e. Board Orientation – The Nominating Committee shall ensure proper orientation of board members by reviewing and recommending board orientation procedures for new members.

B. Personnel and Finance Committee

a. The Personnel and Finance Committee shall be composed of a Chairperson and a minimum of five (5) additional persons. The Secretary/Treasurer of the agency shall serve as the Chairman of the Personnel and Finance Committee.

b. The Personnel and Finance Committee is responsible for recommending candidates for Executive Director to the board.

c. The Personnel and Finance Committee shall recommend compensation of the Executive Director and evaluate the work of the Executive Director annually.

d. The Personnel and Finance Committee shall also serve as the Audit Committee. It shall recommend the hiring of an independent certified public accountant (CPA) as auditor. The Audit Committee shall also review and approve the audit financial statements. It shall also be the contact for the auditor with regard to any illegal acts or fraud, which may come to the auditor's attention, as well as any findings regarding internal controls. The Audit Committee also serves as the primary point of contact for any employee who suspects that fraud has been committed against the organization by one of its employees or board members.

e. It shall develop, review periodically, and recommend to the board, personnel policies governing employment conditions in the agency, including the grievance process for hearing appeals of employees against any violation of personnel policies.

f. The Personnel and Finance Committee shall be responsible for recommending to the Board of Directors policies and plans governing management of the financial affairs in carrying out the services of the agency.

g. It shall be responsible for participation in the preparation of the budget and shall be responsible for presenting the budget to the Board of Directors.

ARTICLE VII

DISSOLUTION

Upon dissolution of this organization, all of its assets remaining after payment of all costs and expenses of such dissolution shall be distributed to organizations which have qualified for exemption under Section 501(c)(3) of the Internal Revenue Code, and none of the assets will be distributed to any member, officer, or trustee of the organization.

ARTICLE VIII

AMENDMENTS

The bylaws or any part thereof may be altered or repealed by a two-thirds vote of the total board membership at any regular meeting of the Board of Directors of the [ORGANIZATION NAME], provided that any proposed amendment has been submitted in writing to each board member at least ten (10) days before said meeting.

_____   _____

President   Date

ACKNOWLEDGMENTS

I am thankful for the inspiration, encouragement, and assistance of many persons in writing this book. I've had the privilege of learning from incredible mentors, community leaders, students, and volunteers whose words of wisdom and experience laid the foundation for a career that sometimes has felt more like a calling than a job.

I'm especially grateful to the Board members, Executive Directors, and Community Development Support Association staff, some of whom took the lead in creating the organization and others whose creativity and commitment have sustained and expanded contributions in achieving local objectives. Also, thank you to the Caring Communities Support Center Board and staff for helping numerous communities in central Oklahoma to establish and strengthen community planning and action initiatives. I am incredibly grateful to the many volunteer leaders, community partners, and professional colleagues whose commitment, determination, and talent made this all possible.

I'd also like to thank my editor, Heather Hollen, book designer, Carl Brune, and cover designer, Nancy Sander. Their creativity and diligence helped me bring the book's vision to life. Thanks to colleagues Sharon Neuwald, Dennis Poole, Brandy Smith, and Randy Barnett for their support throughout the process.

Finally, a very special thank you to my wife, Nancy Sander, and our children for their steadfast encouragement and support for sharing the stories, knowledge, and community local empowerment strategies that have grown from my experience in the last fifty-plus years. I am deeply grateful for their love and support.

ABOUT THE AUTHOR

Gary Theilen, PhD, is a community organization consultant with over fifty years of experience working with local leaders and communities to take action to improve health, education, and income security outcomes throughout Oklahoma. He received his master's degree from the University of Oklahoma School of Social Work and his doctoral degree from the University of Pittsburgh International Development Education Program. Dr. Theilen currently resides in Edmond, Oklahoma, with his wife, Nancy.